To Rosalie and Pov
with Love

Len Frier

No Wall Too High

NO WALL TOO HIGH

A real David and Goliath story

Len Frier
Paige Wilhide, Editor

Mill City Press, Minneapolis

Mill City Press, Inc.
322 First Avenue N, 5th floor
Minneapolis, MN 55401
612.455.2293
www.millcitypublishing.com

ISBN-13: 978-1-63413-304-3
LCCN: 2014922900

Cover Design by Lori Walek
Typeset by Mary Kristin Ross

Printed in the United States of America

CHAPTER ONE

The courtroom walls were stark, whitewashed with a generic shade of flushed ivory. And the pews in the gallery were rigid and uninviting. It was all just as I remembered. Same barren walls, same marble floors, same overhead fluorescent lights illuminating the scene, even the same hard-nosed judge. I watched from the gallery as the case before mine was wrapping up. Anxiously, I thumbed through the piles of paperwork in my lap. I glanced to my right where a stoic Melvin Weinstock, my trusted lawyer and confidant, was biting his lip. *He seems nervous. Should I be nervous? I am a little. But should I be more nervous than I am?*

Before I had time to bother my mind with answers to these questions, the case in progress was dismissed, and the judge announced the next case on his docket.

"MET versus the Occupational Safety and Health Administration."
I'm up. I'm next. This is it.

Just as I was about to stand and make my way to the front, Melvin laid a firm hand on my shoulder. "Let's go. I'll take care of this," he assured me.

He made his way up to the bench on the right side of the courtroom, the one reserved for the plaintiff. When the government attorney from OSHA settled into the defendant's side, they were sworn in.

Judge Joseph Young was a tough, uncrackable force in the courtroom. As a former infantryman in World War II, his military training was reflected in his powerful command of all who stood before his bench. I admired Judge Young, more for his unyielding respect for the American judicial system than anything else.

While I watched all parties ease into their places in the courtroom, I was struck with a moment of déjà vu. I had been in this same position five years prior, in the midst of an arduous journey against the U.S. government, listening intently as Judge Young ruled in my favor. I thought then that I had won my case. *The fight is over*, I thought to myself, struggling to conceal my elation. But as I would come to discover, that was not the case. Now I sat in Judge Young's courtroom once again, watching him read the court documents and scowl in the direction of the lawyer representing OSHA.

"This is the same case I presided over in 1982, is it not?"
"Yes, Your Honor, it is," the OSHA lawyer replied.
"And both parties reached a settlement, did they not?"
"Yes, Your Honor, they did," he answered, almost robotically.

"And now Mr. Frier and Mr. Weinstock are claiming you did not abide by the agreement to allow independent testing labs to operate on a national scale."

The lawyer remained silent, and neither Melvin nor I needed to do any talking. Lucky for us, Judge Young knew the case well.

I was the founder and owner of an independent electrical testing laboratory called MET. We tested products to appropriate safety standards in accordance with U.S. law. In the local Baltimore community and surrounding jurisdictions, we had an upstanding reputation. But in the larger national marketplace, MET faced severe opposition. At that time, the only testing company approved by the government was Underwriters Laboratories, also known as UL. They tested electrical products and approved them for safe use in the home and workplace. Essentially, they operated as a monopoly, and the government allowed them to do so since their inception in 1894. It wasn't until I ignited the issue that anyone even knew of the monopoly. But regardless, I hadn't received much support from other labs, my colleagues, and especially the government. Suing the government was the last thing I wanted to do, but it turned out to be my only option.

Now, here in this courtroom, in the tenth year of my battle against Federal Government, I was exhausted and beaten down. The judge was, once again, leaning in our favor. He didn't hide very well his anger and frustration with OSHA, a frustration I had felt for almost a decade. The courtroom match of ping-pong continued, and I felt more and more confident that we were going to win this one again.

After today, I will have my victory, a victory not only for myself and my business but for free-market trade in any industry. After today, I can finally rest knowing I fought this uphill battle and came out on top.

This is the end, I thought.

It wasn't.

CHAPTER TWO

When I was seven years old, my father packed his bags and left us. He abandoned my mother, my brother, and me. He wasn't even much of a superdad to begin with. Up until he left for good, he faded in and out of our lives, and I never considered him a significant part of my upbringing.

My mother worked tirelessly to take care of me and my brother. She rented a house on Fairmount Avenue in East Baltimore. The top floor had two bedrooms, which we rented out to men who came to Baltimore for temporary work. We lived on the second floor, and my mother converted the first floor into a small dry goods store. We sold socks, underwear, candy, cigarettes, and anything someone in the neighborhood might need. The store allowed my mother to earn a meager living while still looking after me and my brother. There was another store on the block that sold nearly the same items, but they had a fountain, and this propelled their popularity in the neighborhood.

So my mother got creative. She opened up packages of cigarettes and gum, and started selling them for one cent apiece. People who didn't have enough money to buy a whole pack would come to our store to buy single units. They were happy with saving money, and my mother would earn twenty cents on a pack of cigarettes that she used to charge fifteen cents for.

I admired her business sense. My mother was tenacious and determined, much of it stemming from her Russian upbringing. At fifteen, she left behind her parents, three sisters, and one brother, walking from her home in Kiev to Poland during the height of the Bolshevik Revolution. When she arrived in Poland, a Jewish agency arranged for her and others to escape from Russia to Canada, eventually making their way to the United States.

She ended up in Chicago where she met my father and later moved to Cleveland where I was born. We lived in Cleveland briefly, but in the thick of the Great Depression, when money was hard to come by and jobs were sparse, we needed to move where there was work. And Baltimore had work. So we moved to Baltimore when I was just three months old.

My mother was very religious, holding strong to her faith and enforcing the morals that Judaism taught. So for two dollars per week, she sent us to Hebrew school in addition to the free public school education we received. Two dollars was a lot to pay for additional education when she was fighting to put food on the table each night. But my mother tried to protect us from knowing her struggle. And for a while she succeeded. I didn't even realize we were poor until one day at Hebrew school when the Rabbi approached me.

"Your payment is overdue," he chided. "You cannot continue lessons until you bring in the money. You must go home and come back when you have the payment."

It was then that I saw our situation in another light, and I knew my mother needed financial help. So began a string of entrepreneurial endeavors that would sow the seeds for my future in business.

At nine years old, I found an old broken baby carriage in our alley and transformed it into a wagon. Refrigerators were the latest luxury item at the time, a privilege reserved for only the most affluent families, so most homes simply had an icebox that used large blocks of ice to keep food cold.

I walked to neighborhood homes to take their order and collect money to pay for the ice. Then I walked three, four, or five blocks to the icehouse to pick up the ice; loaded it onto my wagon; and lugged the heavy blocks back to the house to deliver it. The ice came in twenty-five- or fifty-pound blocks, too heavy for my nine-year-old self to lift alone, so I required someone to be at the house to help me lift the ice out of my wagon and carry it into the house. This process sometimes took me over a half hour, and the most I received was a five- or ten-cent tip. I quickly learned that this wasn't lucrative.

Down the street from our house were three barrooms and several more a few blocks away. The men who stood at the bar sipping alcohol were always willing to get their shoes shined. Maybe the shoeshine business will be more profitable, I thought. So I fashioned a shoeshine box and invested in some black and brown polish. When the bars were busy, I went down the street and used my shoeshine box to shine men's shoes while they stood or sat at the bar, and they would drop ten or fifteen cents in my box or an additional tip when I was done.

Much more profitable than delivering ice, the shoes took only about three minutes to shine, and I earned ten cents for polishing a pair of shoes and about fifteen cents for boots. Things were looking up. I even found some loyal clientele at the local bars within two to three blocks of our house. This became my territory. I cornered the shoeshine market in this area, and other kids that had a shoeshine box did not infringe.

Eventually, I looked into other pursuits. The penny pinball machine was a big moneymaker in our store. Many kids would congregate around it after school and on the weekends and play it. The machine we had was real finicky and tended to break down a lot. Each time the machine broke down, my mother would call the owner who would send in his mechanic to fix it, and I stood by watching him carefully. When I felt that I understood how to fix the machine myself, the owner to give me a chance to fix it. He opened up the machine and watched as I assessed the problem. To his surprise and satisfaction, I found the problem and fixed it right away.

After that, I went along with the machine owners to other stores that reported broken machines and fixed those as well. After observing the mechanic fix our machine so many times, it was a matter of common sense to me, and the owner paid me a small amount for my service. Eventually he decided to sell off his machines. He was getting older, and the machines too often broke down. As a reward for my hard work fixing the machines, he let us keep the one in our store and two others that broke down too often. Now that we owned the pinball machines, we did not have to split the money anyone, and my mother got to keep all the earnings. But the machines needed to be moved frequently to offer a variety of games for the kids who played them. The games made good money, but moving them regularly would require a mover and a truck, too much of an investment for us, so I sold them to someone in the business.

These are my early memories, working odd jobs here and there to bring in extra money for my family. Unlike most of my friends, I was constantly pursuing activities that earned us some money. My older brother sold newspapers, and I did all types of odd jobs. I never had the time to play ball or any other sports after school. But I never felt left out or different; I had inherited my mother's determination, and it was my responsibility to take care of my mother in any capacity.

School became a burden for me. I attended school reluctantly and wasn't a good student, mainly because most of the time I was bored. At fifteen, I failed the ninth grade for a second time.

It seemed like a waste of time to repeat the year, so I transferred to a vocational school to learn a trade.

"I think I know what trade I want to take," I chirped to my mother when my transfer to Edison Vocational High School came through.

"And what would that be, Len?" she humored me.

"Auto mechanics."

She scratched her chin, impressed by my fervor. "Len, that's dirty work. You don't want to go into a dirty profession. How about you apply to electricity shop? Electricians always have work."

What came off as a suggestion was, in fact, an order, an order that I wouldn't dare argue against. So at her request, I applied to a *cleaner* trade in electricity. I was fifteen when I first attended electrician classes, and for the first time in my life, I was eager to go to school. I became the teacher's pet. I excelled. And I truly enjoyed it. As summer approached, I leafed through the paper every day, looking for a full-time job. An ad titled "Electricians Helper" caught my attention on the grounds that no previous experience was required. Most ads asked for experience.

I got the job, but it was quickly evident why they were looking for an amateur: it required little more than an average man's hand-eye coordination. The work was done in a very large housing project where all the houses were exactly the same. I was instructed to drill holes in the ceiling joists and studs as an electrician followed behind to pull the wires through the holes I drilled.

"I think I can take on some more responsibility, like pulling some wire or something," I suggested.

"You know where all the holes go, and we need you on that job," the electrician explained.

I was grateful to be hired, but I had been drilling holes for almost three months, and I wasn't learning anything. I got out of school for summer vacation in June, and it was now September. Thirsty for more diversified electrical work, I kept an eye on the classifieds.

That September I turned sixteen, a pivotal milestone of freedom for any teenage boy, I was finally able to get my driver's license; and just like any other sixteen-year-old boy, I had itching aspirations of flying down the street behind the wheel of a hot rod with a shiny new paint job. The only problem: I didn't how to drive, and I couldn't learn how without a car.

When I was ready to buy a car, I knew exactly where to go. Many of my older friends in our neighborhood were sprucing up junk cars. They would pay anywhere from twenty to one hundred dollars for these cars and would work on them for days to get them running or just looking good enough to sell.

I found a car for thirty-five dollars. It was a 1936 Dodge, bruised with dents and lacking a front seat. But the car ran well, and for someone who had an affinity for fixing things, that's all I needed. I bought the car from one of the older guys on the condition that he would teach me how to drive.

I got to work fixing up the car. If I was going to use this car for my driving test, it would definitely need a front seat. I found a wooden crate that had been used to deliver oranges to the store. I secured it to the floorboards with the strongest twine I could find. The crate was long enough to reach across the entirety of the front seat, driver's side to passenger's.

For two days, I practiced driving the car in abandoned parking lots, making U-turns, stopping and starting, and changing gears. I felt well prepared for my driving test, but the dents still screamed that the car was in fairly poor shape, and I was desperate to make a good impression on the driving moderator. After all, my future employment depended on his final assessment.

A few hours before I was scheduled to take the test, my friend and I drove to Western Auto and purchased a can of black paint. Black was the obvious choice to make the dents as inconspicuous as possible. In less than thirty minutes, my precious Dodge was smothered in a new coat of black paint, which, I have to admit, didn't look all that great, but it was a decided improvement.

We rushed over to the Department of Motor Vehicles just in time for the test. The paint was still tacky to the touch, so we took care when getting in and out of the car. The examiner, however, was not forewarned of the car's condition. Immediately upon opening the passenger side door, he grimaced indignantly at the sight of black paint blotting his palm. From the driver's seat, I blushed with humiliation at my lack of foresight.

"I'm so sorry. I should have told you——"

"It's fine," he interrupted, displeasure rampant in his tone. "Just . . . just drive around the course. I'll watch from here." He pressed his clean hand against the window of the door and slammed it shut.

I put the car into gear and wove through the course, peeking into the rearview mirror at one point to see the examiner perched on the sidewalk, black-handed, and still grimacing. I felt good when I completed the course and returned to the starting point, but was worried about the poor impression I had made on the guy with my fate in his hands.

The examiner motioned to me to roll down my window.

"Park the car and come inside," he barked. "I'm passing you."

Filled with a combination of relief and skepticism, I didn't ask any questions. I was grateful to have passed, if for no other reason than the DMV gentleman didn't want to see my face or my freshly painted '36 Dodge ever again.

What mattered was that I was now the proud owner of an official state of Maryland driver's license. I was ready to get a job, and I was no longer limited to the streetcar line.

Proving my mother right, there an abundance of jobs for electricians and electrician helpers. The classified section of the *Baltimore Sun* was saturated with such ads, all requiring prior experience. I immediately got a job as an experienced electrician's helper owing to the fact that they didn't ask me about my experience. Even though experience was something I lacked, I learned very fast. I worked beside an electrician each day, learning more about the industry and gaining valuable skills, enough to be able to branch out on my own to do simple electrical work for people in the neighborhood. It seemed like everyone had some kind of electrical work they needed to be done. My name got around, and my positive reputation snowballed, bringing about hoards of new customers. My brother had just joined the navy, and there were no longer tenants occupying the extra rooms in our house. So this steady stream of income put us in a comfortable financial situation and greatly pleased my mother.

Moreover, it satisfied me to be making a name for myself in a respectable and enjoyable trade. What I had learned in electrical shop class was coming alive for me and made sense once I could apply it to real situations. I quickly advanced from being an electrician's helper to an electrician. I earned more money and bought a better car. Still a used car, but any car that had a front seat and a professional paint job was an obvious upgrade from the last one.

Having a car offered me more professional opportunities. I could pack some supplies in my car when I went out on a job, and I would get paid extra for using my car. One job sent me to the supply house of Dorman Electrical Supply, one of our major suppliers for electrical equipment. I simply needed two boxes of wire that came in a fourteen-square-inch box that was about four inches thick. The counterman was very friendly and eager to fill my request as he scurried into the back warehouse in search of this wire. Ten minutes passed, then fifteen. Once twenty minutes had gone and the counterman had not reappeared, I crossed behind the counter and into the warehouse. What I saw there was, for lack of a better word, a horrible mess. Shelves that stretched to the ceiling were bursting with boxes of rolled wires. Some wires tumbled out onto the warehouse floor in tangled and confused bunches, leaving little room in the aisles. And in the center of the chaos was the poor counterman who obviously had to tackle this mess every day.

"You can't be back here," he asserted, rather politely.

"Well, I was waiting over twenty minutes. And now I see why."

"I've found the correct wire. But Mr. Dorman cannot see that you're back here. We don't allow customers in the warehouse."

I paused for a moment and got a brilliant idea that I could help sort out the wires. Working in an electrical supply house would expand my knowledge of electrical equipment, I thought. It was an opportunity I couldn't pass up.

"May I speak with Mr. Dorman, please?"

The counterman found my wire and had me follow him up to the store. He then took me to Mr. Doman's office, sat me down outside of the closed door, and said, "Here you are. You are on your own."

I waited outside of Mr. Dorman's office until he emerged.

"Hi, I'm Len Frier. I'm an electrician, and I work for Mike Price."

"Hello, Len," Mr. Dorman greeted me with a skeptical eye and firm handshake. "What seems to be the problem?"

"Oh, no problem, sir. I was just wondering if you have any open positions in your company."

"You need a job?"

"Well, I would really like the opportunity to work for you and learn about electrical supplies."

"Sorry, son," he scowled, "we're not hiring."

"Please, Mr. Dorman. It looks to me like you really need help in the warehouse."

"Do I have to say it again? We're not hiring."

I scrambled for another approach. "The mess in the warehouse—it's inefficient and leaves customers very unhappy. I waited almost thirty minutes for one box of wire."

His ears perked up.

"If you hire me," I continued, "I promise to straighten out the mess."

"You're a brave boy," he said. "That's a lot to take on."

"Yessir," I stood tall, confident that I was gaining his respect. "I will have it all straight and organized in six days, or you can let me go."

He took a long pause. "Ok, I'll hire you. But you sort those wires out, or you're gone, you understand?"

We shook hands on the agreement. I gave a few days' notice to my boss and started working for Dorman Electric Supply. I got to work the first thing Monday morning, sorting, organizing, cataloguing, and labeling every wire and every box in that warehouse. There were well over a thousand boxes of wire in different sizes and colors spilled all over the warehouse floor. .

Each day for a week, I woke up before the sun, drove the forty minutes to Dorman Electrical Supply House, and dizzied myself with this wire-sorting task. It wasn't much less monotonous than drilling holes, but the professional benefits were invaluable.

It took four full days to finish this project, two less than I had promised; and when I did finish, Mr. Dorman was ecstatic. I had solidified my work ethic and dedication to reaching goals. He was so pleased that he moved me to the counter to wait on customers, a new position that came with a raise and the privilege of meeting a large network of contractors in the Baltimore area. Here and there, I received job offers from some of these contractors, but I was waiting for the right opportunity. After all, it was 1953, and I was earning thirty five dollars a week. At this time, it seemed like an enormous amount of money. And working at the counter offered me the experience of learning about the industry. I soon knew electrical supplies better than many experienced electricians.

I was becoming valuable, and I set my sights still higher. I wasn't sure exactly what I wanted, but I knew I wanted make more money and I wanted a challenge. Drilling holes wasn't a challenge. Sorting wires wasn't a challenge. Neither was selling electrical supplies at a counter. I was rarely motivated by the dollar signs, drawn instead to work that would push my abilities and quench my desire to succeed.

At seventeen, I had a full-time job at Dorman's, and I could finally help my mother move off Fairmount Avenue. I drove my mother through Northwest Baltimore neighborhoods, affluent ones, neighborhoods with sprawling front lawns and towering oak trees peeking out over shingled roofs. My mother fell in love with a three-bedroom home in Park Heights. It wasn't the fanciest house on the block, but it was within our budget. And most importantly to her, the neighborhood was predominantly Jewish. She yearned for me to be surrounded by more Jewish influences: synagogues, Hebrew schools, friends, and especially girls - Jewish girls.. Marrying within our faith was important to my mother, something she persistently encouraged.

So we sold our East Baltimore house for the down payment on our new home in Park Heights. I was excited about the move and the new neighborhood. There were many new people to meet there including Jewish girls.

I became quite fond of one of the girls who often visited her friends in the neighborhood. Her name was Marcia. She had a full head of brown hair that swept just below her chin and a smile that made me weak. But what I noticed first were her legs. Marcia wore short shorts with legs that went on for days. That was a major turn-on for me.

We starting talking and quickly became good friends. The more I got to know her, the more I liked about her. She made me laugh, and she was more intelligent than the other girls in the neighborhood, not just great looks. Marcia's senior prom was coming up, and to my delight, she asked me to take her. As we danced to the band's slow dances in the middle of the gym turned dance floor, I asked her to go steady. She agreed, and that was the beginning of our relationship.

Her house became a new home to me. In the following months, I spent many hours there with her mother, father, and two sisters, exchanging stories over deli dinners and just spending our free time together. We had lots of friends, and her house is where many of us congregated.

I knew Marcia was the woman I wanted by my side for life. I scraped together enough money to buy an engagement ring, and I asked her to be my wife. "This ring is huge," she exclaimed, as I slipped it on to her delicate finger. It was slightly less than a carat, but it was enough that we were now engaged. "I have to go tell my family."

She rushed over to her house as I watched through the window, her mother and aunts and sisters all admiring the ring and joyously embracing each other, their faces wet with tears.

Meanwhile, my professional life was taking off. Contractors from all over Baltimore were getting to know me on a first-name basis. I learned about their businesses and families. And with my vast knowledge of the equipment, everyone seemed to want to hire me. I had a choice of nearly every open electrician position in Baltimore, but one job in particular caught my attention. A field superintendent who worked for one of the largest contractors in Baltimore, MS Butter Incorporated, approached me to work as purchasing agent for their company. I was offered an office in their large warehouse and the opportunity to deal with supply houses and job superintendents directly. I graciously accepted this job and started almost immediately. I sat next to the company estimator, Bill Miller. It was his job to outline all the materials needed on a project and determine the cost of these materials. He knew electrical construction inside and out. I thought this may be a next step for me to advance in this field as the pay was better, and the estimator generally got a decent bonus when the job was successful.

It was during this time that Marcia and I got married. She was eighteen; I was twenty. It was a catered affair with lavish arrays of peach and white roses and over one hundred guests. Marcia came from a big family: her mother was one of seventeen; so between all the aunts, uncles, cousins, and siblings, her wedding party consisted of seven bridesmaids and dozens of guests while my side of the family was my mother and my brother.

"I'm so proud of you, Lenny," my mother said to me, following the ceremony. "You've got a great Jewish woman, and you'll make a wonderful father and husband."

I blushed, "Thanks, Mom. I hope I don't let you down."

"Let me down? Don't talk nonsense."

I said, "Because I can't help you with money anymore. I have so many more finances."

"I know, dear." She squeezed my lapel. "Don't worry about me. Just be a good husband and take care of your wife."

My heart broke a little. I felt like the worst son to have to tell my mother I couldn't provide for her anymore.

"I'll start working again," she continued. "I found a job in a clothing factory, and I can take in the neighbor's dry cleaning." I'll never truly know how much my mother struggled. I also have to admit that I wasn't as good a son then as I should have been. When I look back on my early years, if there's one thing I'm sorry for, it's not being able to provide better for my mother.

Marcia and I went on our honeymoon with the cash gifts we received at the wedding. In those days cash gifts were common; five or ten dollars in an envelope was normal. Our first night, we sat up counting our money so we knew how far we would be able to go.

The gift I received from my boss Charlie Buttner was much more generous than most: a raise to $100 per week. When we returned from our honeymoon, we rented our first apartment: a one bedroom in a private home. The owners had built a separate entrance to our apartment on the second floor, so we would have private access. It was the perfect first apartment, but we both wanted to have a family and knew a one-bedroom would be too small for children. Marcia became pregnant in no time and gave birth to our first daughter, Cheryl, one week before our first wedding anniversary. This apartment worked until Marcia got pregnant again with our second daughter, Susan. We finally managed to upgrade to a three-bedroom house in a very nice part of Baltimore, an ideal neighborhood to raise children. Almost everyone around us was about our age with small children. The house cost $7,250, and the monthly payments were $65 a month.

We bought it just in time because soon Marcia was pregnant again with our third child, this time a son who we named Robert.

It was in this small house that I would start my business. I would spend many nights working in a small six-feet-by-six-feet storage room in the basement. The house represented so much more than just another purchase. It was the beginning of my future, paving the way for what would be a thrilling, and often frustrating, career.

When we had settled into our new home, I found an ad in the classifieds that caught my attention: "Electrical Draftsman/ Design Engineer—work in engineering office developing electrical drawings." This ad didn't mention experience or other qualifications, so I applied over the telephone and very briefly told them I was a purchasing agent for a large electrical contractor and I would like an interview. To my surprise, I was granted an interview right away.

Going into the interview, I felt anxious and shaky. Although I didn't expect to get the job and it wasn't critical that I be hired, I was exploring the possibilities. I dressed neatly, black slacks and a freshly ironed button-up dress shirt, but I felt so out of place. Through the glass window where the receptionist sat, I saw people walking around the office wearing ties and suit jackets. There's no chance for me here, I thought. The nerves were eating away at me, and all I wanted to do was walk out of there, but I stayed to see it through.

A very well-dressed man came in to get me for my interview. He politely and reassuringly introduced himself as Ernie Siegel as he escorted me back to his office.

"Have a seat, Leonard." He gestured toward the chair as he poured me a glass of water. "So what makes you think you're qualified for this job?"

"Well, sir—"

"Please, call me Ernie."

"Ernie"—I cleared my throat, incredibly uncomfortable with that request—"I trained at Edison Vocational School as an electrician."

"Yes, but what experience do you have in the field? This job requires a lot of knowledge about drafting and preparing electrical drawings. Can you do that?"

"Yessir, err, Ernie. I have to prepare electrical drawings as a purchasing agent in my current job," I lied. I had no experience with drafting or electrical drawings.

"And you feel comfortable doing it on your own if were to assign you a project?"

"Yes, I definitely can," I lied again. I didn't feel comfortable at all doing that.

"Tell me, Leonard"—he leaned back in his chair, inspecting every expression—"you've gone from an electrician's helper to an electrician, to a counter man, to a purchasing agent for one of the largest electrical contractors in such a short period of time. How have you climbed the ladder in so quickly?"

"Well, sir, I'm a hard worker. I am driven to learn as much about this field as I can. And because of that, all my bosses have really liked me." I surprised myself with how confident I sounded.

"Ok, young man, wait here for a moment. I'm going to speak with my supervisor."

He left the room. I took a big sigh, realizing I probably hadn't been breathing for the entire interview. In the past, my interviews consisted of the other person simply asking if I was interested in the position. This was very new for me, and although I felt a little guilty about lying, I knew I could learn what I needed to learn.

Thirty minutes passed, and Ernie Siegel returned.

"I'm giving you the job on hunch, but I feel good about you," he said with a smile. "The job pays $75 a week, and you'll start next Monday. Is that OK?"

"Yes, that's wonderful." I stood up and shook his hand. "Thank you so much. I really appreciate it. I won't let you down, promise."

On my way home, it sunk in that I would be making $25 less per week than my current position, and even worse, I had to break this news to Marcia. I knew she wouldn't be happy. At the time we had two children and a house with a mortgage payment of $65 a month and Marcia was pregnant with our son Robert. I prepared what I would say to her and practiced the speech on my drive home. "I'll pick up side work to make up the difference, Marcia. We'll be fine." Though I already did plenty of electrical jobs on the side, my only goal was to put her worries at ease.

And as most of my decisions worked out, we had to do a little suffering in order to get through each day, which sometimes meant having no food in the house. Luckily, Mr. Cooper, was one of my best customers and the owner of a local delicatessen. He always needed something to be fixed or had a small electrical job for me. When he saw us walk into Cooper's Delicatessen at suppertime with our three children in tow, he knew I had no money. At these times, Marcia and the kids would eat dinner in the deli while he came up with some work I could do to pay for the meal. The trunk of my car was full of electrical supplies and tools so that I was prepared for most anyype of small job. After I finished my work, I ate a quick sandwich. All the waitresses knew us and our kids. They sat and played with the children to pass the time and gave each child an animal cracker-sized box of cookies to take with them when we left. We were all happy and very appreciative. We felt blessed that we were able to get through each day, one day at a time.

CHAPTER THREE

The night before I was to start my new job, I couldn't sleep. I stayed up most of the night worrying about everything from being late the first day to making an irreversible mistake that would completely shame my reputation and the company. Marcia kept telling me to stop worrying, but that was like telling a child not to cry. I didn't know what to expect. I knew I'd have to wear a tie to work every day. I knew working with engineers and other professionals would be very different than working with electricians. I knew that most of the engineers and designers were college educated. How would I fit into their world? I took comfort in knowing Ernie Siegel had hired me and he wouldn't hire just any average Joe.

That morning, I arrived at the office at seven thirty, a half hour before I was told to be there. For a full thirty minutes, I stood across the street watching the door to the building, thoughts and worries rushing through me.

At precisely 8:00 a.m., I entered the building and gave my name to the receptionist.

"Welcome, Leonard," she said with warm enthusiasm. "It's

nice to meet you. Just wait a minute. I'll find Ernie and tell him you're here."

That welcome was such a relief for me. I felt better.

"Hey, Leonard, great to see you again." Ernie Siegel approached me in the waiting room, just as well dressed as he had been during the interview.

"Great to be here," I responded.

"Well, let me show you around." He glanced down at my hands, which were clutching a brown paper lunch bag. "Did you bring your pencils?"

My heart started racing. "No, sir. Just a lunch. I didn't know—"

"That's fine," he interrupted. "Usually engineers bring their own mechanical pencils, but you can borrow some from the company."

He gave me a brief tour of the building, introducing me to anyone we happened to meet in the hallway; then he took me to the office where I was to work. It was a fairly large room with two big drawing boards, separated in the middle by a large desk and a big glass window that looked out into another much bigger office. One of the drawing boards was perfectly clean, and the other was covered in sheets of paper and one large drawing. Sitting at the desk was a man dressed, of course, in a suit and a tie.

"This is Eaton Bayor, our chief electrical engineer," Ernie said, "and this is where you'll be parking yourself." He pointed to the clean board and the chair in front of it. "Make yourself at home here, and I'll leave you in Eaton's capable hands."

My very own drawing board. I couldn't believe it. Was this really my job?

"So tell me a little about yourself," Eaton inquired. "First, how did you get this job without some training or experience as a draftsman?" He was a very refined man; his English was impeccable. I later learned he was a graduate of Virginia Tech.

"I don't know, except I guess Ernie figured my other experience was valuable and he could train me to be a draftsman."

"What kind of experience *do* you have?" He was genuinely interested in hearing about my previous work, and I was excited to tell him. So we spent most of the morning talking, as my anxiety slowly melted away to excitement.

That afternoon, he gave me a book on lettering. We unrolled some paper on my board, and he showed me how to draw a straight line. Never before had I thought I needed to be shown how to draw a straight line, but I did.

"The key," Eaton explained, "is to turn the pencil as you move so the line doesn't get wider as it moves down the sheet."

I drew a few, what he called guidelines; and from the book, I practiced lettering.

I spent the next few weeks learning the ropes, how everything operated. In our engineering office, a team consisted of an electrical engineer and a mechanical engineer working together; it was truly a team effort. I learned that the architect would furnish the engineers with the floor plans of the proposed structure. This included all electrical and mechanical requirements. Then the electrical and mechanical engineers worked together to design the heating and air-conditioning system, the plumbing, and other mechanical components. The electrical engineer then designed the power requirements and connected all the mechanical equipment. It all had to be coordinated very closely.

As the chief electrical engineer, Eaton taught me a lot about the theoretical end of the work. He would sketch a layout or design that I would transfer to the drawing, and in return I taught him the practical stuff: how the equipment we were drawing plans for would actually be installed. We had a good partnership. He appreciated my input and was pleased to turn over some design work to me while he concentrated on writing the specifications. I picked up everything very fast and impressed the people I had to impress. It wasn't long before I received a raise from $75 a week to $85 a week. I knew Marcia would be pleased with the extra ten dollars a week, but it didn't cover the additional money we needed.

The mechanical engineer on our team was Hank Schlinger. A mechanical engineering graduate from the University of Maryland, he was incredibly skilled, and as a team we worked well together. It wasn't long before Hank and I became good friends. I remember many mornings we spent carpooling to work together, talking about our families, and giving each other career insights. On one of those drives, he said flat out, "Len, I'm looking for another job. The pay is just not enough for me and my family to live comfortably."

"I know, Hank," I responded. "I had to take a pay cut from my last job to work here. I've been looking for more opportunities too."

The conversation quickly escalated, and we decided to offer ourselves to companies as a team. Together, we were fast, efficient, and did impeccable work.

It didn't take long before we got a few bites from companies. After tedious research, Hank decided that we could do best at the firm of H. Walton Redmile & Associates, and without even an interview we were hired, sight unseen, for $25 more a week than we were making at our previous job. Needless to say, Marcia was very happy about that.

The projects they did were very large and more complex. The firm handled projects like Baltimore Memorial Stadium and the new Maryland State Office Building. These were high-profile projects, and I was making contacts with some important people in the industry, contacts that would come benefit me in the future.

Additionally, Redmile didn't care if Hank and I accepted

design projects on the side, so we were able to work for architects in the evening or even other engineering firms after our regular hours. Most of Redmile's projects were very large, so there was no chance of us competing with Redmile. We both developed a relationship with a small architectural firm: Morris Steinhorn and Associates. They handled projects such as small shopping centers, churches, and synagogues, projects that took us only about a week, working each night, to complete.

It wasn't long before I was appointed as the field electrical engineer, overseeing the construction for the new fifteen-story Maryland State Office Building and six-story State Roads Building being built in Baltimore. This made me feel incredibly accomplished. I had been at Redmile for a short time, and they trusted me with two huge projects. I couldn't have been prouder of how far I had come.

Redmile's main office was in Bethesda, Maryland, and the office in Baltimore was a branch office. When Mr. Redmile decided to consolidate the two offices, he needed to keep the Baltimore office open while the state building was under construction. It was necessary to perform construction inspection, and Redmile's contract required these inspections. In addition to keeping current in changes to the building as agencies were moving in, I did the construction inspection. Therefore, everyone in the Baltimore office, except me, moved or traveled from their home in Baltimore to Bethesda, a one-hour drive. I'd made this trip a few times a week but didn't like it.

Since many different agencies moved into the state building, there were numerous electrical changes that needed to be made to satisfy each agency's department head. That was my new job at the Baltimore location. Regularly, I met with various state officials to discuss their needs and incorporate their electrical requirements in revised drawings. I got to know many of these state officials very well.

All dealings with the state of Maryland required the involvement of Garrett Billmeyer, the top nonpolitical civil servant at the State Department of General Services. He was, in short, a very important person. He signed the contracts on state construction, handled all bidding, and I dealt with him on a regular basis concerning the state office building changes. After a while, he became a sort of friend of mine.

While working on the building and doing my inspections, I realized that the state didn't have an electrical inspector for new state construction. They relied on the design engineer or code officials who did electrical inspection on new construction but only for code compliance, not state contract compliance. I saw an opportunity here and decided I would try to become the state electrical inspector. But first, I needed to convince them that there was a need for this position and that I was the man for the job.

Architects and engineers specify good-quality electrical components such as receptacles and switches to be used when building. There are basically two choices of components: those that cost one dollar each or those that cost five dollars each. The better receptacles or switches are more dependable, can take abuse, and last longer. They both work and are both recognized by Underwriters Laboratories. This means they would both be acceptable to any inspection agency. The difference, of course, is quality. The five-dollar units are worth the price, and the one-dollar units will do the job and still be approved by the code authorities. But the state paid for the higher-quality devices, and they would be cheated if the lower-priced ones were installed. Only inspections for contract compliance would be concerned with the lower-price device being installed. Once the wall plate was installed, it would be difficult to see the difference.

I approached Colonel Billmeyer and asked him about providing inspections on state projects for determining contract compliance in electrical installations.

"That's a great idea, Len." He responded with enthusiasm, "Draft up a proposal to the state, and I'll support it."

Colonel Billmeyer was aware of my knowledge of components and devices since I had worked as a purchasing agent for a contractor and an electrical supply house. Being recommended by Colonel Billmeyer almost assured an automatic approval. So with his blessing, I wrote a proposal to the state of Maryland to perform contract compliance inspections, on a contract basis, on new state construction.

The proposal went to the Board of Public Works, and I waited anxiously for it to be approved. Winning this contract would mean I would now have a reasonably good and dependable income from the inspections, and it would be the perfect opportunity for me to risk starting my own business.

The next hump—and a big one at that—was to run this by my wife, Marcia. Too often I'd make a personal decision without first talking to her, which didn't make things too pleasant at home. But I was impulsive and had to do things immediately. If we discussed things first, often she'd disagree; but if I did it first, I felt she'd have to go along.

In this case, starting a business was different. There was big risk here since I'd have to leave my job at Redmile; and we had three children, a mortgage, plus other expenses. All these issues left Marcia worried, and there was nothing I could say to reassure her. She was very practical, and I was not. I was impulsive, ready to try anything I felt could work But I am only thankful that she seeded to my wishes.

I incorporated my business, Maryland Electrical Testing Company Incorporated, in October 1959 before the contract was awarded, hinging on the hope that it would happen.

This allowed me to write the proposal under the name of Maryland Electrical Testing Company. That's who the contract was awarded to. I'd done a huge amount of part-time work over the years, and this was the first time money that would be paid to an official company. I had to go through the process of getting a bank account, printing stationery, etc. It felt good.

During my inspections and my dealing with many electrical contractors, I saw a great problem contractors were having in getting a high-voltage installation tested to be sure that they are safe. High-voltage installations are necessary in buildings that require a very large amount of electrical power such as hospitals, office buildings, or university campuses. In order to buy this kind of power, the owner must install a high-voltage system, and prior to being energized, it must be tested. At this time, there were only two companies that performed these tests for the contractors: General Electric Company and Westinghouse.

The problem was that these companies would only work on a per-hour basis and wouldn't commit to a firm quote to perform the tests. Contractors always need firm quotes from suppliers; it's the only way they can estimate the costs of the project. Also, testing work must be coordinated with other trades or with the utility and a firm schedule is a must. GE or Westinghouse wouldn't commit to a firm schedule either.

I called my new company Maryland Testing rather than Maryland Inspection because I saw a need for competitive testing in Baltimore. The idea of being in this testing business sounded good to me, but I wondered how I could pull it off. It wasn't like I was competing with just any company; these were two of the largest companies in America. If they wanted, they could squash me in a second.

Except for a few of the engineers I worked with, I didn't know any business people; and I really didn't want to talk about this with anyone, not because I thought they'd steal my idea but because they might belittle it. The only one I know whose opinion I could respect was Ernie Siegel from Green Associates. If it was really a bad idea, Ernie would point it out.

So I scheduled a lunch meeting in a restaurant around the corner from Green Associates. My old employer.

As soon as we ordered our food, I got down to the matter at hand.
"Ernie," I said, "I've got an idea for a business, and I want to bounce it off you."
He sat back in his chair, crossed his arms with power, and said nothing.
I continued, "You know that in any electrical system when high-voltage equipment is installed testing is required."
"Now don't tell me you're thinking about doing the high-voltage testing," he interrupted.

"Yes, don't you think that's a good idea?" Ernie looked puzzled. "After all, there are only two competitors, and neither Westinghouse nor GE is customer friendly."

"I would not want you to do something that could hurt you financially, Len." I could hear the bits of apprehension in his words. "First, the test equipment is expensive and has to be maintained. So expensive! And why would any customer give you a job when they may need to go back on the company if their testing wasn't done correctly?"

Before I could gather the words to respond, he powered on. "Of all the businesses you could go into, Len, this would be at the bottom of the list."

I felt a little discouraged. "Ernie, I really respect your opinion, and I'll have to think about it. I know there's a risk, but I think it's a small risk; and if there's any real risk there at all, I don't see it."

"Don't get me wrong," Ernie said. "I would be happy to invest in any business you plan to go into but not in this business because I say it would be a failure."

"With all due respect, Ernie, the idea of testing is sort of exciting and challenging to me. I don't want to say it's a dream that I must follow, but I feel that I must pursue the idea more before just trashing it so quickly."

"Well, good luck, Len. I'll do what I can to support you, and I hope it works out."

Leaving that lunch without Ernie's approval was discouraging, but I knew this was a business I wanted to pursue. So I decided to also talk to another trusted friend Hank Schlinger about my plans. So I met with Hank and laid out the idea.

"Len, I don't know if that's such a good business move. Have you considered the downside?"

I had but maybe not to the extent I should have.

"Also, what's your plan to purchase the equipment? It's very expensive. Do you have the money to buy all this equipment?"

And do you have insurance to cover your risk? It's really a big risk!

Of course, he was right, but again, I didn't see the risk. All I would be doing was apply a test voltage to a piece of equipment that couldn't damage anything.

"And without insurance, if you make a mistake, you'll be paying for the mistake the rest of your life."

That was a point I hadn't considered. What kind of insurance would I need? How much would it cost? Would this be the end of my business?

"Len, do you have a lawyer?" he continued.

"I don't. Why? Do you think I need one?"

"Absolutely you need one. If I can give you any advice, it would be to hire a lawyer. And I'd bet that he'll tell you exactly what I'm telling you right now: the risk is just too great."

I said, "Hank, I know your intentions are to help me, but I feel comfortable with what I'm doing, and I don't feel the risk is there."

"Well, do it, and if I can help, let me know; but I want you to know that you're attempting to climb a huge wall going into competition with Westinghouse and GE, where contractors will realize they have an entire company behind them and you have no one. I hope you are not making a big mistake."

I was a bit discouraged, but my determination overcame all doubts, and with that I ventured out into the uncharted world of electrical testing. After all, didn't everyone tell the Wright Brothers that they couldn't fly? Well, they ignored the masses, and look how that ended.

And I knew there would be a demand because testing a large system is so important. Let's say the electrician makes a mistake or a bad part is installed. In a home or even a large building, when that electrical switch is first turned on, the circuit is interrupted, the problem is found, quickly fixed, and there's no damage. After finding and fixing the problem, everything works normally.

This, however, isn't the case in a large high-voltage electrical system. A fuse or circuit breaker on these systems only limits the damage. There can still be unnecessary damage to the extent of a fire or an explosion at the point of the problem. Because of the complexity of this extremely expensive equipment and the power contained in the circuit, it all must be tested before it is turned on. The testing simulates the voltage being applied by starting with a very small amount of power. If a problem existed, we could determine that problem while causing no, or very little, easily corrected damage to the system.

The importance of high-voltage testing wasn't an issue, and neither was the demand. Back when I was on the counter at Doman Electric Supply Company and as purchasing agent at MS Buttner Company, I constantly heard about issues with the contractors needing to get testing done. But it wasn't until I started working in the engineering field that I understood the problems.

My first plan of action was to talk to these contractors. I printed business cards and visited the contractors to tell them about my business. I didn't have to introduce myself. Most of them already knew me from the counter at Dorman Electric or as the state of Maryland electrical inspector, so I was always very well received.

I also stopped by the local "dodge" office, the central hub where all drawing and specifications are filed and available for inspection when a job is out for bids. All vendors of electrical equipment go there to find out if any items they sell or represent are specified so they can provide quotes to the contractors. I began visiting the dodge office to see if high voltage was part of any project and if testing was specified. Often testing wasn't specified because it was just understood, and there wasn't a need for it to be specified.

It didn't take me long to find a newly awarded job that needed lots of testing. The project involved replacing and modernizing the high-voltage electrical distribution system at the U.S. Government Printing Office in Washington DC. The contractor was EC Ernst Company, based out of Washington DC.

I knew this job was perfect for me because it only involved high-voltage cables, not transformers, which would have required a lot more testing equipment.

So I called the project manager on the phone and told him about my services. "It is really a relief to hear from you," he started. "I can't tell you how fed up I am with GE's pricing system. I must say I am a bit skeptical, though. You say this is your first major testing project?"

"Well, yes. But I assure you that I have all the test equipment required and can do the job to meet the government requirements"; and before he had time to pose another concern, I added, "Plus, I can quote you a firm price. I know GE and Westinghouse can't say the same."

"No, you're right on that one." He paused for just a moment. "Ok, Len, I like the way you do business, so I'm going to take my chances on you. How about you send me over a proposal, and we'll get to work?"

True to my business model, I sent over a firm price, which I later found out was dirt cheap, but he accepted. Then reality started to marinate in my mind, and several issues arose. I didn't have any of the testing equipment that I'd need or the money for it. I would also need a truck to move the equipment. The project manager hadn't mentioned insurance, and neither did I, so I still didn't know how to approach that hurdle. But of all the things I didn't have, I did have the job and the confidence to do it, and I was headstrong and determined to get it done better than the other guys.

I saw this as an opportunity, and I wasn't going to let money, or lack thereof, stop me. I found a company in New York State that made the equipment I needed. I contacted them and found out the prices for a high-voltage test set for testing cables. This and a few other items of equipment that I could pick up used in Baltimore were all I needed.

During this whole process, I was sure of one thing. If I had told Marcia that both Hank Schlinger and Ernie Siegel advised me not to go into this business, she would have ended it then.

So I had to be real shrewd. I would tell her things like "Marcia, I can't believe no one has thought of this kind of small business yet" and "I'm the only one who's doing this. It's such a great idea and a fantastic business opportunity."

I really wasn't that smart to fool her, but I guess she just trusted me. I'm just glad she didn't know the entire story at the time.

So I scraped together enough money to pay half the cost of the test set and offered to pay out the rest with time. The company accepted this arrangement, so I placed the order and sent in my deposit. My plan was to drive my car to New York to pick up the equipment. That was until I discovered that the equipment, with oil, weighed over four hundred pounds. If that wasn't enough of a problem, the tank for the testing unit had to be filled with special insulation oil and couldn't be laid on its side, forcing me to rethink my means of transport. The scheduled day for the testing in Washington was fast approaching, and I needed a truck, and I knew I wasn't going to get it in time.

It seemed that everything was needed at once. The test set was planned to be finished on a Wednesday. The manufacturer would fill it with insulating oil in order to test the unit, then drain the oil out so I could put the test set in my car. Hopefully I could drive back in my car Thursday night. In the meantime I asked one of my brother's good friends who owned a filling station if he'd look around and buy a truck for me. I needed a half-ton panel truck at my house on Friday when I got back from New York so I could purchase a fifty-five-gallon drum of Univolt 33, the insulating oil I needed in my transformer.

The four-hundred-pound test set was on wheels, but it was too much for me to move on my own. I needed a helper, so I enlisted help from my neighbor Al. The cables were installed in the project but needed to be connected and tested after power was turned off in the building, so the testing needed to be done at night .

Together, Al and I loaded the test set onto the old Chevy panel truck for the trip to Washington DC. I wasn't worried about the test itself, but I was really worried about making the journey. The truck had a lot of wear and tear, loaded up with lots of miles, and afflicted with lots of loose parts and rattles.

That trip took way too long. When I heard a strange noise, my heart skipped a beat. I kept saying to myself, "Please don't break down. Just get us to the job."

"Don't look so concerned," Al reassured me. "We'll make it there." I couldn't help it; it was in my nature to worry.

When we finally pulled into the parking lot at the government printing office, I felt a huge weight off my shoulders. To me, the hard part was over.

The testing went as smoothly as expected. We unloaded and connected my equipment and proceeded to perform the testing under the watchful eye of the project engineer and a government inspector who were there to witness the testing. After about eight hours of continual testing, the job was finished.

"I was really impressed with your work, Len," the project engineer told me afterward. "When GE or Westinghouse comes in, they use older equipment that fails half the time."

If I'd known in advance that one or both of them would be

at the site to witness the testing, I'd have been more worried; but now, hopefully, word would get around that there was a more reliable company than GE or Westinghouse. And I couldn't have been happier. I was almost as happy as I was to show up on time without suffering a breakdown on the road.

I could hardly wait to start work on the test report when I returned home that morning. I'd seen test reports from GE or Westinghouse; and they reflected no details on the testing methods, equipment used, test readings, and in some cases, they were handwritten, leaving much to be desired. I understood that the test report was all most people would see of me. If they compared my test report next to one from GE or Westinghouse, they'd be impressed and, hopefully, select me.

In addition to providing firm quotes, these test reports were my marketing plan that would make MET different from the competition. In business everyone needed a marketing plan; this was mine. I worked two nights to finish the test reports and submit them, and with the test report I also submitted my invoice. Now I was really happy.

CHAPTER FOUR

In electrical contractor circles, word got around that there was a new company providing testing services and quoting firm prices for testing projects. Previously, this type of business was unheard of. The idea caught on; and I was very busy issuing quotes, performing tests, and writing reports—I did everything. Although the issue of insurance still weighed on me, it hadn't come up with any contractors, so I didn't see the need to address it.

That was until I bid on a small testing job for the U.S. Army at Edgewood Arsenal in Maryland, the first job that wasn't for an electrical contractor. I was the successful bidder; actually, I was the only bidder. GE and Westinghouse didn't want to risk time over this estimate should they discover that additional testing was required. The government doesn't enter an open-ended contract with anyone.

When I placed the bid, I did not read the bid documents completely. It wasn't until I was scouring them later that I found out the army required all contractors on a military installation to furnish proof of insurance.

I worried the required insurance would be similar to malpractice insurance, in that it would cover the cost of anything that could go wrong on a large power system, an unbelievably expensive insurance policy. If that turned out to be what was needed, I would have to say goodbye to my business and let GE and Westinghouse do it all.

This could be the end of Maryland Electrical Testing Company, I thought.

"This could be the end of my business," I vented to Marcia after dinner that night. "I just don't see how I can afford such a large policy if that's what I need."

"Wait and see what the insurance might cost. Don't look at the worst-case scenario, Len."

"But all I can think about is how much would it cost if I did something wrong and shut down the entire Edgewood Army base. Plus, I'm only getting $500 for the job. Is it even worth it?"

"Be optimistic, like you usually are," she assured me. She was good at bringing me down to earth when I needed it. "Wait until tomorrow when you learn what's required."

The next day, I spoke with someone in our home insurance agent's office about business insurance, and I was relieved to discover that the government only required workman's compensation insurance coverage. It was cheap, so I bought it sight unseen; and that was that, even though I was the only employee. But that wouldn't last very long.

I soon hired several technicians, full-time and part-time, since a lot of the work had to be done at night or weekends. It gave me a great opportunity to find real talent who had full-time jobs and wanted extra part-time work.

Hiring more employees allowed me to increase our capabilities as the requests for additional tests came in. I didn't want there to be a test on electrical equipment that we couldn't perform. And more than that, I didn't ever want to say that there was a test that we couldn't do because we didn't have the equipment.

This policy caused lots of grief for some of my employees. Instead of doing what we had the ability to do and enjoy our advantages, I constantly pushed for additional capabilities and invested in new equipment. This wasn't just any equipment; most of the equipment we needed was special and required our own engineering, design, and building to perform these special tests. There were very few companies in the United States that did this type of testing, so no equipment manufacturers were enticed to enter this business. If I needed something that wasn't commercially available, I had to build it myself, unlike GE and Westinghouse who already had massive factories to build their equipment for them.

I did all the engineering for the design of the equipment. I subcontracted out everything I couldn't do myself. The rest, the wiring and installation all the interior components,

I did at home in my basement. I taught myself to do everything in building this equipment except fabrication of the enclosures. This metal work required special equipment to form, shape, and weld the enclosures. What I needed was a factory with a fabrication shop and occasionally some engineering help, especially in designing and building special transformers.

This metal fabrication work was done at a Baltimore company called Powercon Corporation. They were a relatively large manufacturer of large electrical equipment, the same type manufactured by GE and Westinghouse. Although they were competitors of GE, Westinghouse, and other manufacturers, they had a good working arrangement with all of them and often manufactured equipment for them. They did most of the testing on the equipment they manufactured, and only on rare occasions did they need us. However, I often needed them to manufacture the metal enclosures for me. As a test laboratory, we didn't need a lot of supplies or other purchases since we mostly sold labor.

I would often visit the Powercon plant when I needed a small metal item or an electrical part that wasn't sold in the local electrical supply houses. During these visits, I developed a relationship with some of the company's most skilled workers. The president of Powercon, Ralph Siegel, didn't mind if I used some of his people to help me with some of the projects I was building. Occasionally, we would use some Powercon's machinery after work hours to do special fabrication.

"Are you sure you don't want me to pay you to use your machines?" I often asked the president, Mr. Siegel.

"Just wait until you have a really big job"—he would laugh—"because then I'll soak you."

Powercon's president wasn't only a prince to me but a true friend and a philanthropist. Once, a local Boy Scout troop came to the factory asking for a donation so they could buy a small trailer for camping and moving some of their supplies around. Ralph asked the scout leader to tell him what kind of trailer they wanted and that Powercon would build them the best trailer they could ever imagine. I was there the day the scouts came by to pick up the trailer. It was truly a touching moment. That is the kind of person Ralph Siegel was.

In 1968, Ralph Siegel called me into his office to ask for my help. This surprised me.

"Len," he said, "I've come up with a great new metering system."

I listened intently. It wasn't every day that Ralph Siegel asked for my advice.

He continued, "It can be used wherever there are multiple tenants in a facility without submetering."

"Well, sub-metering isn't legal in many places, so it makes sense," I said. "How would it work?"

"It would be a simple system that would allow the owner to

estimate the electrical usage of a tenant without connecting a meter."

In Maryland, like most states, only a regulated utility company is allowed to sell electricity. It prevents companies from cheating buyers or users out of electricity. However, it is legal for a person to estimate a charge for electrical usage and charge the user that amount. This would be common in a large complex, for example, where the rent includes the utilities.

I knew this was serious because Mr. Siegel was a smart guy and a good businessman. I knew that if he needed something he would try to build it himself rather than buy it. And if he needed some special talent, he'd hire it. Why would he need me? I couldn't imagine what was involved with making the device, how it would work, and what kind of special testing it would need. Most of the testing needed by Powercon, he'd do himself. He had many extremely smart electrical engineers who could come up with any special tests that might need to be done. At first I thought he wanted me to invest in this device. It sounded good, but I didn't have any money to invest, and I'm sure he knew that because I was often a little late in paying his invoices. All this ran through my mind when I asked what I could do for him.

"So what are you asking of me? Do you want me to invest? Because you know I don't have much—"

"Oh, nothing like that, Len. I think I can do more for you here than you can do for me. See, I have two customers that would like to buy this system, but they told me the device will need approval by Underwriters Laboratories."

"Ah, I know a little something about them." I remembered hearing about Underwriters Laboratories, or UL, from the connections I made when performing inspections for the state. "They're an independent laboratory like MET, right?"

"Correct, and I've been talking to them for the past six months. Turns out they make it extremely hard for new products to get onto the market."

"How so?" I was intrigued.

"Well, they don't know anything about my product, how it works, or what's required to test it—and they don't care. But because I'm the manufacturer, I can't test my own product. They said that they'll find a standard that fits the product and test to that standard. If no standard fits, they'll have to write a standard that applies."

"That sounds like a complicated process," I said. "How long could that take?"

"Up to a year, but we can't do the testing. The testing can only be done by an independent laboratory. This brings me to you. Since you're an independent laboratory, you should be able to do this work."

"I don't know anything about the product, and I'm sure we can do the testing, but I wouldn't be able to supply a UL label," I said.

"Well, try digging around," Mr. Siegel suggested, "and find out what's required to apply a UL label."

After a bit of research, I learned that UL was founded in Chicago in 1884 as a "not for profit" company, completely independent of any manufacturer, supplier, or producer. Their initial tests were done on fire equipment and later grew to include electrical inspectors. They test electrical products in accordance with product standards that they write, and only after UL's acceptance can an electrical or fire protective device be legally installed in the United States. After they finish their investigations, they allow a manufacturer to apply a "UL" label, denoting that the device has successfully passed their tests.

I had recently been approached by the American Council of Independent Laboratories (ACIL) about joining their organization, and to help Mr. Siegel find out what is needed to receive a UL label, I thought ACIL would be a good place to start.

I called and spoke with their executive director, Douglas Dyes. "Could you tell me whether UL is a member of ACIL?" I asked.

"Well, they can't be; they're a not-for-profit organization," he explained. "In fact, our organization is very much against UL because they are unfair competition to some of ACIL member laboratories."

"You mean they're a monopoly?"

"Exactly. And ACIL is absolutely committed to ending all unfair competition to its members including government and academic laboratories that compete with tax-paying ones."

"So what might happen if I called UL, asked if I could run a test for them, then applied their label to something I tested?"

"Good luck," he said.

I felt frustrated. How could I try to work with this monster corporation that doesn't even know I exist? Then Mr. Dyes went on to suggest another solution, "I think it would be in your best interest, Len, if you join ACIL and help us oppose UL. What do you say?"

"Let me do some more research and get back to you," I said.

The issue was weighing on me. How could one company have so much power in the marketplace? Was Douglas Dyes right about all this? And if so, how would that affect the growth of my business?

The best way to get information is to talk to people firsthand. So the next time I ran into one of the electrical inspectors I knew, I asked him about the UL label.

"Most inspectors I know, myself included, can only accept the UL label on a product," he replied.

"What if I could create my own MET label and get inspectors to accept that?" I inquired, confident that I could make my way into this marketplace.

"Seeing as the electrical inspector is usually the final

authority on the matter, I think it would be rare for you to get just one inspector to accept a MET label."

With that, I agreed that the most effective way I could oppose UL's operation was to join ACIL. That clinched it; I joined the next week. Little did I dream that this would turn into a battle I'd be fighting for the next twenty years and change the direction of my life and the future of Maryland Electrical Testing Company.

I returned to Powercon to tell them everything I'd learned. "Mr. Siegel," I said, a bit uneasy to deliver the bad news, "like taxes, you're stuck. UL is in total control of the electrical testing industry, and all you can do is go along."

We were both discouraged, and in the end, Powercon never manufactured the product. I never found out what it was, but knowing Ralph Siegel, I'm sure it was something of great value. He forgot the project, but I didn't.

I wondered how a monopoly could operate in the United States with impunity and with no one stepping forward to end it. When only GE and Westinghouse were performing high-voltage testing, that was a competitive issue, not a monopoly, not a complete obstacle to providing a commercial service. This really bothered me, and I wondered what I could do to break the UL monopoly. I quickly realized that by myself I wouldn't be very effective.

This convinced me to join ACIL and became active and knowledgeable with this issue.

When I first joined, all the testing done by my company was performed in the field. We brought our testing equipment in a truck to the site. Almost everything we tested was part of, or related to, large power systems. None of this testing work needed a laboratory.

But testing products in a lab really sounded better than traveling all around the country. I didn't have any regrets about field testing; I just thought testing products in a lab was more ideal. And why should only one lab be allowed to test certain electrical products? I was angered by the unfairness.

I felt that my involvement with ACIL would provide me with an opportunity to develop my own electrical testing laboratory. I kept looking for an area of testing that I could get involved in. The laboratories involved with ACIL included chemical testing, lighting laboratories, physical testing laboratories, mechanical testing, and environmental testing. I was very interested in these laboratories. Though we didn't perform these services at the time, I felt that nothing was out of the question.

The only type of testing laboratory that was not represented was electrical testing due to UL's reign over that industry.

But I figured that if an opportunity developed to open an electrical testing laboratory, being at ACIL would help me find out.

ACIL was very involved with the U.S. government with regard to issues relating to testing laboratories and approvals or recognition of testing laboratories. They had regular meetings with officials at the Federal Communication Commission, the Federal Trade Commission, the Justice Department, and others. These agencies used ACIL's input when developing testing requirements for private telephones, televisions, or voice communication devices. Many of these commercial electronic items were being imported and needed to meet U.S. requirements for compatibility with U.S. systems. Another big issue was the restraint of trade issues with imported products. These were all important issues that ACIL was instrumental in developing solutions to solve.

I didn't get very active with ACIL at first. I received frequent notices of meetings but rarely attended because they always seemed to include a government agency that at the time didn't interest me. What interest would I have in the Federal Trade Commission or the Federal Communication Commission? I did think that the Justice Department would be of interest in breaking the UL monopoly, but I never saw them listed for a meeting.

All my industry connections were involved with electrical power equipment, and that was the field that made most sense for the evolution of my business. I spoke with my friend Hank, telling him that I really didn't see any real opportunity to develop a laboratory with just my field testing.

"You have to connect with a group of laboratory-testing people if you want to find an opportunity to get into the laboratory business," he said.

"How do you expect me to do that?"

"By being around people connected to electrical power equipment. You're a member of ACIL. Why don't you go to one of their meetings and see who you can talk to? If an opportunity does develop, that's where you'll hear of it first."

So when the next meeting notice came, I went. The meetings were at the ACIL offices on K Street in downtown Washington DC and chaired by the executive director of ACIL with one of their attorneys. (Some labs insisted that an attorney be present so no one could ever claim that collusion occurred at the meetings.) I met the executives from most of the large labs in the United States. I found out that even the large labs had less than fifty employees.

The government's main agenda was to promote trade—all kinds of trade—and they didn't want any issues or practices that may restrict trade. Most of the concerns that arose involved standards. The government's concern was that standards were transparent and open. My concern was the

UL monopoly on approval of electrical products did not allow another lab to enter this business.

As I got more and more involved with ACIL, I become somewhat of a delegate from the United States who traveled all over the world to meet with governments and conformity assessment people. Our goal was to harmonize standard requirements and ensure that U.S. products were dealt with on the fair and equal basis as the products of other countries.

I hoped this continued involvement with ACIL would eventually lead to a system or solution that would break up the UL monopoly. To me, breaking up this monopoly was akin to breaking segregation. How can one group of people exclude another group of free people from entering a business or entering an establishment or providing a product or service in a free market? If nothing else, I wasn't going to let this monopoly go unchallenged. Little did I realize what I was getting into.

CHAPTER FIVE

My field testing business was progressing smoothly and rapidly. I subscribed to a service that advertised when large projects were out for bids. Most often these very large projects which needed high-voltage equipment such as transformers and high-voltage cables. I'd find out where the plans and specifications were available for potential bidders, go look at the plans, and determine if testing was required or specified.

If there was a high-voltage system where testing wasn't specified, I'd get the name of the engineer and go meet with him. I'd tell him he should be specifying testing and give him some sample specifications. I'd then get the names of all the electrical contractors bidding and quote a price to everyone for all the testing as required so they could include my price in their bid, and they wouldn't have to guess at what the testing might cost. If they worked with GE or Westinghouse, the price of testing would be a guessing game.

Eventually, I didn't have to go to the dodge office or meet engineers anymore; the contractors started calling *me* for a price on a job. Sometime the successful contractor didn't get a call from me with a price during bidding, but after they won the bid, I followed up to be sure they were aware I had a price for the job. Some jobs never came out for public bids. Sometimes jobs weren't advertised, but dodge had the specifications. Then there were jobs for private bidding, by invitation only. Some private owners didn't want everyone involved. But the state or federal government had to allow public bidding. This mainly happened when a company did or didn't want a union company as a contractor. Because I made an effort to bid on all jobs where testing was required, most contractors sought us out.

MET's business kept expanding. We expanded west to Pittsburgh, Pennsylvania, south to Virginia, and everywhere in between.

For about five years I had two full-time technicians at the Norfolk Naval Base and other naval facilities in and around Norfolk, Virginia. Twice I received a commendation from the navy in Norfolk that came with an engraved plaque that I have hanging in my basement: one from the naval facilities in Dam Neck, Virginia, and one from the Norfolk Naval Base. We also had contracts to test at two nuclear power plants: the Muddy Run nuclear power plant in Maryland and the Beaver Valley nuclear power plant near Pittsburgh, Pennsylvania.

I also discovered another untapped area of testing in load

testing diesel-driven electric generators. These generators provide emergency power to critical installations, such as hospitals or important defense installations, and they ensure that the generator will carry the emergency load of power during an interruption of electrical service. Identifying a problem with a generator is critical for engineers, and the only way to correctly test any generator installation is with an artificial load bank that approximates the load that exists in the facility. This involved simulating a large load on the generator equal to 100 percent of its rating and then a 110 percent overload, applied for over eighteen hours to identify any problems that could develop on the generating system.

To do this testing, I had to manufacture one of the largest items I've ever worked on: a load bank. It was built in our newly rented three-thousand-square-feet facility, an old garage that I'd modified with an office, large shop, and storage for out-test equipment. For three months, I would escape to the facility in the evenings and on weekends, constructing this load bank on a four-wheel heavy-duty trailer. All the wiring and final assembly I did myself. I only sought help when assembling the heavy items. When all was said and done, the finished piece of equipment weighed over three thousand pounds and was the largest single item of equipment we owned.

One day we received a call from Fairbank-Morse Company in Milwaukee, Wisconsin.

"I'm looking to load test a very large generator to meet military standards in our plant here in Wisconsin," the gentleman on the other end explained. "Would your company be able to perform that testing?"

"Sure," I replied, excited to have another prospect for this branch of our business, "we have a lot of experience doing generator testing, so let me fax you over a quote later today."

"Thank you so much! You wouldn't believe how difficult it is to find this kind of testing. I've been on the phone for two days calling all over the country, and you were the only ones with the capability."

This wasn't the first or last time I heard a comment like that, and it made me proud that our company was getting recognition for its range of services, and more importantly, our scope was spreading to the Midwest.

The job at Fairbanks-Morse happened to be in the summer when our three kids were out of school. At the time, the kids were eight and six and three, and taking them to Wisconsin seemed to be the only way all five of us could go away on a vacation. So Marcia and I decided to go to the Wisconsin Dells for a vacation. I didn't know much about the Dells, but the client said it was the best place for a vacation in that area of the country.

I equipped our new 1969 Chrysler station wagon with a tow package for the load bank and other trailers. We folded down the rear seats and laid out a thick quilt in the back of the station wagon for the kids (seatbelts had not yet been invented), loaded the equipment, connected the load bank, and we were off. Traveling on a vacation with our kids, pulling a three-thousand-pound trailer was not an ideal way to travel, but we both realized that we have to take what we can get. Needless to say, we got a lot of attention for it when we were on the road getting gas or buying lunch. Strangers would often approach us and ask, "What is that thing?" I know lots of wives that would not have accepted this as a vacation, but Marcia was understanding and accepting of this lifestyle. I was (and still am) so grateful for that. For the entire twelve-hour drive, the kids played and slept in the back. When we got to the motel, we settled in, and the next morning I took the load bank to the job site and left Marcia with the kids.

Testing generators using our large load bank was very profitable. We probably could have charged more than we did, but the price was fair. In addition to the load bank, I had to furnish many heavy cables. I always asked for an electrician to work with me and connect them. It was more expensive than any other service we provided. I estimated the time at about $150 per hour for testing time, plus travel and setup. I usually was the one that went on these tests, mainly because I'd built the load bank and knew how to handle any problems, which happened often. It gave me an opportunity to take Marcia and the kids on some mini-vacations around the country.

So when we got a call to quote load testing a very large generator for launch pad 38 at Cape Canaveral, Florida, I jumped at the chance. There were other generator supplier companies that were able to do this test, but they needed to join many of their smaller load banks together to reach the capacity. My three-thousand-pound piece of equipment won me the job!

I had another advantage in that an ex-employee of mine, Chuck Ruhl, had moved to Coco Beach, Florida, for work. We had communicated often, and he said that if I ever had a need for someone there, he'd probably be available. He was an excellent electrician, an even better technician, and a great person to be around. Usually, when I got electricians from a customer, they were nothing special; they would wait for an instruction and couldn't do anything without being told first. When I got the job, I called Chuck up, and he was happy to take the job. I couldn't have gotten someone better to work with me on this test.

After a while there were no tests on an electrical power system that we didn't do. Financially, though, I was never really ahead. I was constantly buying or building new testing equipment, and because of this, the collections lagged behind the expenses and investments. And I admit I didn't always make the wisest investments. Sometimes I would spend a thousand dollars to buy a piece of equipment (or build a piece of equipment myself) to do a job that occurred infrequently and didn't cover the cost, and I didn't even know what a "cost-benefit analysis" was at the time.

But to me, these jobs moved us forward because we were one of the only companies that could do it, and that's what was really important. Our growth and expansion were tied to our ability to constantly increase our testing capability. Most companies hired us because we had the ability to do the required tests, not because of our prices. So if we intended to grow, we needed to have the ability to do any test that might be required.

We expanded to perform maintenance testing of high-voltage equipment. Maintenance testing is like getting a periodic medical checkup. By testing your blood or getting an EKG, you would know, in advance, how parts of your body are performing, giving you important information that you wouldn't want to be without. In a way, this is exactly what maintenance testing is. Just like there are many medical conditions for which there are no warning signs, in a power system there are no warnings of an impending power failure.

But it's not like pending failure of an air-conditioner or heating unit when the air-conditioner stops producing cold air or the heating system stops producing heat. In those cases, you feel the failure coming, and it can be fixed easily. A power system is much different; in a power system, nothing makes noises or squeaks or rattles. It just stops, and in an instant there are no lights or critical services. For example, when the main electrical system in a hospital shuts down, after about twenty seconds, an emergency generator will start. But this generator usually only provides essential services. The bulk of the power in a hospital is used for elevators and air-conditioning equipment. These items and other non-essential elements are not usually supplied by emergency generators but are absolutely necessary. Luckily, maintenance testing can easily detect conditions that might cause a complete power failure.

It takes a special knowledge and ability to identify potential problems in the equipment on an electrical system. If someone was interested in money alone, they could enter this business and easily claim work was done when it wasn't. Everything would continue to work after a project was completed. Unless we found and corrected a problem, our service left a system exactly as we found it. Everything runs as before. The difference is to the extent a responsible and professional evaluation will detect potential problems. There are no standards or oversights for the services we provided. This work is unregulated and allows anyone to claim they did the work when they didn't, which was always a problem for me.

One day, I received a phone call from a large electrical company in Dayton, Ohio,

"We are electrical contractors, and our company has an electrical testing division," he said. "I've heard great things about MET, and I was wondering if you're interested in attending a meeting of other companies in the electrical testing business."

"Well, thanks for thinking of me," I replied. "What kinds of issues are on your mind?"

"We really want to discuss problems with the industry and ways the business could be made more professional."

It was an appealing topic to me. "I do feel that there is a need to enhance this type of business into a professional service. You know, this has been on my mind lately."

"I was hoping you would say that." I could hear the excitement in his voice. "Our main goal is to start an association so we can demonstrate to our customers that we can police ourselves."

"Count me in," I exclaimed, and so was the beginning of the National Electrical Testing Association (NETA).

Our first meeting was at a Holiday Inn in Dayton, Ohio, a small association of field testing companies comprised of my company, MET; High-voltage Maintenance Company in Dayton, Ohio, and Milwaukee, Wisconsin; Burlington Testing Company in Burlington, New Jersey; and a company in Hayward, California.

The group's main interest was to increase the credibility of the independent testing industry and develop some standard testing requirements. There weren't any standards, and the five companies weren't uniform in the services they provided. The group was also opposed to General Electric and Westinghouse doing this work because they would make maintenance secondary to the other services they provided. I was 100 percent in favor of these goals.

I didn't know how an electrical contractor could be independent when testing some of their own projects. This did bother me, but I kept it to myself.

Eventually, I became president of NETA and remained president for over fifteen years.

As president of NETA, I traveled a lot at my own expense because I felt the need to promote the industry. Since we were some of the first to pave the road, the responsibility fell on us establish the credibility of the industry. We printed pamphlets illustrating the importance of detecting a problem before it becomes a failure. We also conducted training sessions for our technicians so they could all be up-to-date on the latest technology and testing equipment. We were all relatively small companies and invested a large portion of our time and money to educate the people who were responsible for high-voltage systems. Though these deeds were never officially or publically recognized, I think they were necessary to laying a foundation for the business and infusing the industry with integrity from the beginning.

As I was traveling on behalf of NETA and still growing my business, I kept thinking about Ralph Siegel's project and how the UL monopoly had prevented him from producing a possibly innovative device that would save energy costs. I questioned how this monopoly could exist in the private sector, and if the legal system wasn't doing anything about it, what would it take to end it? Could I do anything to end it? It was obvious to me that I needed more time to investigate this, and now wasn't the time. We had a problem most companies would love to have: we had too much business. This meant I didn't have the time to really delve into the issue, but it didn't stop me from thinking about it. At the time, all I was able to do was think about it.

CHAPTER SIX

Most of our testing clients were electrical contractors that installed high-voltage systems. By the very nature of this work, they were mostly large electrical contractors with special capabilities to handle the high-voltage equipment and have the expertise that was needed.

Our work involved testing the system after installation and prior to being energized and turned on. One contractor with whom we did a lot of work was Mace Electric Company, and Earl Mace was a principal of this company and the son of the owner.

One day, while on a job, Earl and I started talking about airplanes, and he told me that he owned a private airport. This was unbelievable to me. "How can someone who owns an airport also work as an electrician?" I asked.

"You don't believe me?"

"Of course I believe you. I just don't see how you can have the time to do this and run an airport. I barely have time to run my business."

"I make time. Flying is a hobby of mine. It's exhilarating."

I thought about this, and the thought occurred to me that maybe I should take up a hobby. It would ease the stress of the job and get my mind on something else.

As if he was reading my mind, he proceeded, "How about you come by sometime and I'll show you around, and I can take you up for a ride in my plane?"

This was a really exciting offer. I'd flown many times but always commercial. If I was really lucky on those flights, I would grab a seat by the window. But flying private was new to me.

"Yes, I'd love to," I said without hesitation.

I got the directions to the airport and planned to meet him there on a Sunday at nine in the morning. I drove to the airport under a cloudless bright blue sky with just a touch of light wind: beautiful weather for flying, I thought. I followed his directions up a few back streets and looked for a sign directing me to an airport. It wasn't until I made my final turn that I saw a small sign that said Baltimore Airpark. I drove up the driveway, and soon lots of small airplanes started to appear, parked in no particular order throughout the back lot. In the center of the grounds was what looked like the main building, not much larger than a small convenience store. On a hill that was not visible from the drive-in road was a few large metal buildings and a large lineup of airplane hangars and metal buildings. The area was certainly much larger than what appeared from the road.

I parked the car just outside of what appeared to be the main building. Inside was just one large room and a counter for waiting on customers. Along the wall were two ratty old sofas with a few people sitting and chatting with each other. I later found out they were waiting to go flying, some as student pilots and some as the passengers. I found Earl Mace behind the counter.

Earl was there waiting for me. "Ready to go for a ride?" he asked.

"Yes, I'm ready," I said with mounting excitement.

"Excellent. It's a great day for it." A woman stood up from her seat behind the counter. "Oh, Betsy, this is Len who I was telling you about. Len, meet my wife, Betsy."

"Pleasure to meet you." I shook her hand.

"Betsy helps me out with the day-to-day operation. She's in charge of the schedules and money."

"Are you excited to fly today?" she asked.

"I am, I am. Just a little nervous. But I'm really looking forward to this. It's a new experience for me." I felt myself rambling.

"Well, great." She smiled. "You are in Earl's very capable hands, so there's nothing to be concerned about."

With that, Earl and I walked out the back door of the building, and I found myself surrounded by many different types and sizes of private planes. He walked me to his airplane as he explained the different parts of the plane.

"This is a Cherokee model 140. It's a single-engine four-passenger plane with a low wing and four seats inside."

I believed him, although I couldn't see how two people could fit in the back.

There was only one door on the right side of the plane, and Earl had to enter the plane first. Once inside and buckled in, Earl explained what he was doing as we were taxiing. He taxied to the end of the runway and ran to about 1,800 rpm while keeping the airplane from moving. Earl explained that this is always done before any flight to make sure all parts of the engine are functioning. These explanations of all the controls and gadgets helped calm my nerves as we took off smoothly into the crisp air.

For nearly twenty minutes, we flew around, looking down on the city below. I enjoyed the thrill immensely. The landing was just as smooth as takeoff; I hardly felt the wheels touch the ground. We taxied around the airport until he found a spot to park the plane.

"I'll show you how to tie down the plane so the wind can't move it around."

Together we tied down the plane, and I felt like a real pilot, taking care that his precious plane was secure to the ground.

Back inside the terminal, Earl proposed, "If you enjoyed it like it appears you did, you must be ready for a lesson."

"I think I am," I eagerly replied. "Where do I sign up?"

"Talk to Betsy at the desk, and she'll get you all signed up."

I didn't want to leave that day. I spent a few extra minutes walking around the building, meeting some of the other pilots and flight instructors; and on my way out, I stopped at the front desk to talk to Betsy again.

"I heard you're ready for a lesson." She smiled. "Would you like me to get that set up for you?"

"Absolutely. I can't wait. What times do you have available?"

"Well, we've got next Sunday open. How's that?"

"Perfect," I said. "And how much for the lesson?"

She brought out a price chart that outlined all the extras. "Including airplane rental and the flight instructor's fee, it will be eighty dollars for the hour."

It was more expensive than I thought, but I was going to do it. I didn't have any other hobbies, and I felt I was due for something for me.

"Ok, sign me up!"

I couldn't believe it. I was now a student pilot.

I went home and told Marcia that I'd signed up for lessons to learn to fly. It didn't bother her too much, by now she was probably used to my endeavors, and I was happy for that.

This was the only thing I did outside of work. I worked most of the time, and I needed the break.

I arrived that Sunday for my first lesson, and lucky for me, it was another beautiful day. The instructor's name was Jim Ball; he was the chief instructor at the airport.

"Before doing anything else," Jim told me, "we must walk around the plane and check everything." We had to assure that there was no water in the fuel. In order to do this, Jim Ball showed me how to sample some of the fuel from the bottom of the fuel tank.

We had to sample the fuel by removing a small among from under the wing from a small spring loaded valve. If there was water in the tank, it would have collected in the bottom and would be able to visually see. We then tested all the movable surfaces to be sure they were free. And we checked the oil level with a dipstick to be sure all covers were secure.

Bill said, "This is called a preflight walk-around, and it must be done before every flight. This is very serious. Now get in the pilot's seat, and we'll get started."

I didn't expect to be sitting in the pilot's seat on my first lesson. I thought it would be like the flight I'd had with Earl, where he sat in the left seat and I was the passenger. This made me a little nervous.

Jim started by showing me which controls to use and when to turn the key. He then showed me which gauge to look at to be sure the correct setting was set at the start.

He then helped me taxi to the takeoff point, and we were ready.

"Push in the throttle all the way then put your left hand on the yoke," he instructed. The plane had dual controls, and even though my hand was on the yoke, he was right there directing me. "Now the difficult part is maintaining the climb. Even the slightest pressure forward or back will cause the plane to descend or climb."

Before I knew it, we were taking off, and I was singlehandedly flying a plane. Jim directed me to do mostly straight and level flying so I could get used to the plane.

I was hooked, and once a week for the next six months, I went to the airport to take lessons, not just in the air but on the ground as well. We were required to take ground school classes so we could understand the charts that are used when flying. Each chart had hundreds of symbols, and each symbol or marking included extremely important information for the pilot. The charts also contained most of the frequencies that needed to be used when communicating to the flight controllers. There was an awful lot to learn, not only about the airplane but the air traffic system as well, and I had to take all these classes before I could fly solo.

All pilots are required to have forty hours of flying time before they can fly solo. When I took my first solo flight, I had over fifty-five hours. When I completed my flight, a few pilots and instructors were waiting on the ground to award me my certificate. Every pilot gets a certificate when he completes his first solo flight, and I proudly framed mine and hung it on my shop wall. It was a very momentous event for me and the beginning of a lifelong passion.

For the next few months, I visited the airport regularly, renting out airplanes and honing my flying skills. But in the rental plane, I couldn't take a passenger up with me unless he was also a licensed pilot. My goal was to get my own airplane and an instrument rating.

When it comes to laws affecting private pilots, there are "visual" ratings and "instrument" ratings. Visual flight rules require flying in conditions with at least three-mile visibility, and they apply to all new pilots. The more advanced rating is the instrument rating, which allows pilots to fly through clouds or in weather conditions when they can only rely on their instruments. In Baltimore it isn't possible to fly far without an instrument rating; overcast weather can occur quickly, and if you're flying when bad weather closes in, you'll find yourself stranded until the weather improves. I considered myself a cautious pilot, and I never flew when the weather was iffy.

I also spent a lot of time at the airport, talking to other pilots, students, and employees. In no time, I became one of those people sitting on that old sofa that I'd noticed on my first visit. Hanging out there became some of my most relaxing and enjoyable times. I got to know most of the people there. Two of the pilots with whom I got friendly were Frank Lombardo, an electrical contractor, and Hal Piper, a flight instructor and owner of a ground school.

We had tossed around the idea of buying a plane together, and when the opportunity to buy a 1964 Mooney arose, we jumped on it. A Mooney is a high-performance airplane with retractable wheels, and it was a lot faster than the Piper Cherokees I had been renting. Hal negotiated the price, and we all chipped in to buy it.

The three of us being partners worked out well. We seldom had a conflict with each other in scheduling the plane. After about two years, however, I sold my portion and bought a newer four-passenger Mooney on my own. I got serious about my flying and started working on my instrument rating so I could fly in any weather. It took over a year, but I finally got my rating, and the plane became a valuable asset for business.

When we opened an MET office in Pittsburgh and Norfolk, Virginia, I needed to make frequent trips to each of these locations, and the plane became invaluable to the company. After about three years I upgraded again, selling the Mooney for a 1984 six-passenger Beechcraft Bonanza, and that's when I really started seeing the benefits it had for my business. I hired one of the commercial pilots from Baltimore Airpark to fly for me when I had to transport an employee or equipment to Pittsburgh or Norfolk, and I couldn't make the trip for whatever reason.

I flew all over the East Coast but always kept within five hundred miles from home. These flights were never more than three hours and just perfect for small business trips to Pittsburgh or Canada. I really grew to love flying, and it was a great retreat from my general duties. At times, I would fly through overcast skies, but I was mostly a fair-weather pilot; they live much longer anyway.

For a couple of summers, we rented a two-bedroom condo in Ocean City, Maryland. We packed up the car with all our summer clothes, beach stuff, and the three kids, and drove to spend a few weeks at the beach. But I still had work duties. So while Marcia stayed with the kids, I flew home every Monday morning, worked during the week, and flew back every Friday night. One of these sunny beach days, Marcia and I were lounging on the beach as the kids built sandcastles and dove through the waves.

"I've been thinking," Marcia said to me. "What do you think about getting a condo of our own?"
"Like buy one?" I asked. The thought hadn't crossed my mind before, but I was making more money and had extra disposable income.
"Sure, why not? The kids love it down here and think about how much we'll save every summer if we have our own place?"
She was right. New condos were being built all along the ocean. Surely this was one of Marcia's brilliant ideas.

After shopping around, we bought a condo in a new section of the city, close to plenty of shopping, restaurants, and entertainment. It was a cozy three-bedroom and two-bath with a living room, kitchen, and a balcony directly over the beach. The name of the building was the Rainbow, and we bought lots of trinkets with a rainbow on them. It worked so perfect. Everything about this place was perfect: the beach didn't get overcrowded, it was easy to walk up or down as we were on the fourth floor, and our beach neighbors were very friendly. We came to cherish our times at the ocean and felt very blessed that we were able to enjoy it without sacrificing any necessities.

Here is where I really enjoyed my family and the fruits of my labor.

CHAPTER SEVEN

Business continued to expand into other areas of testing and inspections. Just when work was getting good in one area, I would jump into another area of testing that always required more investment.

"Why are you getting into something else when things are starting to look really good?" Marcia would ask.

"How about a little breathing room?" I'd always say. "I can't help it. I'm an entrepreneur."

She would just shake her head, trusting that I wouldn't put the family in any financial danger.

When I see an opportunity, I usually jump in. I can't resist taking advantage of an opportunity when it presents itself. It's like my addiction; I need to keep getting into something new or a previously untapped area of testing.

I find there are at least two types of entrepreneurs: one who needs to do something because of the money that might be made on the venture and the other one, like me, who does it because there's a need or a void, with someone not offering a needed service. I feel that people that do the work for the money are never satisfied. They continually need more money. I'm very satisfied to accomplish something and don't seek anything else. Only when something presents itself do I feel a need to pursue it. Making money or building the company has never been my primary purpose, but it's a good measure of my efforts. I really feel good when someone tells me, "I'm glad someone got into this business" or says, "It's about time someone gave them competition."

Testing and inspecting are very closely related; it's hard to do one without doing the other. At the state of Maryland, building my contract involved mostly inspections, but we performed necessary tests as well. Because the state was doing a lot of construction, we were kept busy with inspection requests.

So to keep up, I was forced to hire another inspector, someone who knew what the inspections involved and also could learn how to help on some other MET projects. Since the state inspections wouldn't take all this person's time, we needed someone with other skills to do more than just inspections.

Before buying an ad in the Help Wanted section of the local paper, I decided to ask around. This is how I found Bob Johnson, an electrical superintendent for a large non-union electrical contractor in Baltimore. Bob was a very good inspector but had difficulty adapting to the kind of test work we had. Rather than let him go, I found other special services he could do with electrical surveys. In the past we'd done some surveys for an engineering firm, which consisted of determining how electrical power was being distributed in a very large complex by recording the power on a few circuits. This provided the engineer information on how they could add additional loads. Because of a previous purchase, I had most of the equipment to do this but hadn't pursued it seriously. Bob was just perfect for this line of work.

For the first time, I developed a flyer soliciting business. I'd never needed to advertise before; the business always came to me through referrals and word of mouth. But the mailings were incredibly successful, and we received so many responses that I had to move one of my young technicians from testing to work for Bob in surveying.

One new client that contacted us from the flyers was the Rouse Company, a company that owned shopping malls all over the United States, and their main office was in Maryland. Rouse and other mall owners didn't design their stores with separate electric meters. This would have a resulted in a very costly electrical installation. Instead, the mall owner was able to buy large amounts of power at a wholesale price per kilowatt hour and then legally estimate the electrical costs to include in the price of rent for retailers; it couldn't be a separate charge.

The Rouse Company hired us to come in and install

temporary kilowatt-hour meters on the electrical supply to each store, which would determine the accurate electrical consumption for the period the meter was installed.

Because tenants could see exactly how much electric they were using, they didn't complain about the cost. This was the legal way an owner of a mall could charge for electric usage, and most tenants accepted these charges. The store was billed the accurate cost they'd be billed if they were connected directly to the utility. And the mall owner was buying the power at a wholesale price and making a profit by selling it retail. After all, it was their business to make money.

We also provided a service to map out a very large electrical distribution system. Often an electrical system was added to or modified after a few years. It's generally not known what is connected to the system in order to know what additional loads can be added. To determine what's connected and what the loads are, we performed an electrical system survey. Our largest customer for this service was the U.S. government. We provided this service at Vandenberg Air Force Base, Great Lakes Naval Training Station, and several other military installations. These surveys rounded out the services offered by MET Company but were still a long way from testing products in the laboratory.

We had developed a lot of businesses, many customers, and a good reputation. We performed testing projects all over the world in places like Spain, Liberia, West Africa, and Greece. We had almost one hundred employees, and we were profitable. By many standards we were a success.

But I still longed to open an in-house electrical test laboratory. I thought about it all the time and hoped an opportunity would develop. I joined the National Research Council after they proposed an investigation into "standards, conformity assessment, and trade in the twenty-first century." Product certification fell under this category, and that's why I joined; I was hoping to influence some action by the government to end the UL monopoly. I thought a recommendation from this influential committee might force the government to end the UL monopoly. That would do it, but I wasn't sure if it would happen on its own. The committee work lasted over two years, and a lot of recommendations followed, but the right agencies in the government did not follow up on many of the recommendations.

Nothing I was doing was moving me closer to the laboratory business. It was very frustrating for me. I was beginning to think I was wasting a lot of my time going to meetings or joining groups that I thought might help me break into the laboratory business. I really was not seeking to put UL out of business. I just want to get a share of this kind of work. I felt we had the ability and knowledge to do some type of laboratory test on electrical products. We just needed an opening—an opportunity.

Most of my efforts did not materialize. But I felt that if an opportunity for laboratory business developed I was in the right place to spot it. I wondered how many entrepreneurs developed electrical or electronic devices but did not move forward to produce the product because they were turned off by what it took to get the product to market. When the government identifies a monopoly, they unusually take some action to end the monopoly, even going so far as to sue the applicable company when their persuasion doesn't work. Since monopolies are illegal, it has to be the responsibility of the government to act. This had been the case, many times in the past, with other monopolies. When would it happen with UL?

CHAPTER EIGHT

The duty of an electrical inspector that works for a city, state, or municipality is to ensure that an electrical installation is safe and complies with the National Electrical Code, the electrical inspector's bible. But even the best inspector cannot simply look at a device and determine whether it is safe. In order to make this determination, the device must be tested to the appropriate standard. In the United States there are national standards that apply to all electrical products. Most U.S. standards are written by Underwriters Laboratories and are publicly available. The standards can be used by anyone who has the technical ability to perform the appropriate tests. However, at the time I was growing my business, the only laboratory tests inspectors would accept was those done by Underwriters Laboratories. After it's confirmed that the product meets the applicable safety standard, a label is placed on the device. This label acknowledges that the device was tested and is correct and safe for the installation.

Most local jurisdictions require all products be listed by a nationally recognized testing laboratory because the label tells the inspector everything he needs to know about the device. The term of nationally recognized testing laboratory was code for Underwriters Laboratories since no one else was acceptable. When an electrical device arrives on a job without an acceptable label by a recognized testing laboratory, the device is rejected and must be removed. The contractor or owner could either replace the device with a labeled device or in some cases call a recognized and accepted laboratory to test it to an applicable safety standard.

This could be exceptionally burdensome and expensive. Even though there are many independent labs with excellent engineers that have the ability to test the device to the applicable standard, only Underwriters Laboratories was acceptable to most electrical inspectors. But some labs got themselves approved by individual and were able to label a product in these jurisdicions.

To become recognized as a laboratory that performed tests on devices in accordance with applicable standards, I turned again to Bob Johnson. He'd worked for a large electrical contractor in Baltimore and happened to be very knowledgeable about the National Electrical Code. He was also active with the local inspector groups and attended local inspector meetings. Since the local inspectors were considered the "authority having jurisdiction" (a term used in the National Electrical Code), we asked to be recognized by the local inspectors for testing products to prove that they complied with the code in our area.

We had the reputation as an independent testing company, and we had the capability to make these inspections, and we were already doing inspections on electrical installations for the state of Maryland. The inspection departments in Baltimore City, Baltimore County, and others soon accepted our approvals and our MET labels on products were accepted. After we gained this recognition locally, we quickly expanded into many other jurisdictions around us.

We set up a department just for these inspections. Soon after, manufacturers started asking if we'd test their products and apply one of our labels so the approval agency would accept the product. This would allow them to sell the product without the need for field inspections but only in jurisdictions where we were accepted.

Field inspections and product testing are slightly different. Though a lot of the same equipment and manpower is used, an approval on a field-tested product only applies to that one product that was individually tested. When testing a sample product, we had to be sure that each subsequent product was exactly the same as the sample—no differences at all. In order for this to be accomplished, additional follow-up inspections at the factory were required. These factory inspections would open up a lot of additional business. All we needed was for other jurisdictions to accept our label. This was more than difficult; at the time, I thought it was impossible.

Underwriters Laboratories had built a monopoly—maybe not intentionally, but that's what it was. There are over ten thousand municipalities in the United States. Underwriters Laboratories was the only organization in the United States that was accepted everywhere. UL was very active with inspector groups all over the country that unquestionably relied on the organization to provide testing. Many inspectors were on UL counsels, advisory groups, and standards committees. Their connections to "authorities having jurisdiction" ran deep and were unbreakable. Underwriters Laboratories, in addition to performing all the safety testing on products in the United States, also wrote most (if not all) of the safety standards.

The safety standards were written by a separate group at UL but under the control of one president. The groups that wrote these standards included the U.S. government, local and federal officials, manufacturers, but mostly UL personnel, all on a voluntary basis. At the time everyone, including me, agreed UL provided a very good and needed service to the general public. And for that they were rewarded very generously. They had piles of business without competition, they named any price they wanted, and they didn't have to pay taxes. What a deal!

If I or anyone else wanted to get into this business, we just had to do what UL did. But we were fifty years too late. Anyone who wanted to get into this business had to be able to convince a major retailer that their label was as acceptable as UL's. But without paying a dime or lifting a finger, UL had thousands of inspectors tell anyone who wanted to sell an electrical product that it's not legal, and if you want to sell your product in any jurisdiction, you must receive UL recognition.

I quickly realized that if I wanted to get into this business, I had to get all ten thousand jurisdictions to accept MET as a recognized laboratory. Not 9,999 jurisdictions but all of them. Would a major manufacturer want to come to MET or anywhere else where he couldn't assure acceptance of his product with a MET label?

The only solution to this, I could think of, is the government declaring UL a monopoly and either closing them or forcing them to allow MET to apply a UL label. This way an inspector wouldn't know who had done the testing. I actually didn't think any of these scenarios would ever happen, but I was hanging on to hope.

If that wasn't bad enough, UL wrote all the U.S. electrical product safety standards. If a product didn't meet these standards or failed one of the tests, it was rejected. Although UL says that there is an appeals procedure, I never heard of anyone using it. A manufacturer had no choice but to use UL and accept their results. If a manufacturer decided to use a lab like MET whose approval was accepted in only a few areas, the manufacturer took the risk of limiting his market. It made perfect sense for a manufacturer to use only UL. Only on a few occasions was a manufacturer willing to limit his sales until he could get his product through UL, so he came to us.

To get into the testing business, I often used the word 'impossible'. That wasn't an exaggeration. The tests are required by not just federal law but also by local laws and ordinances. Local laws wouldn't normally be changed by any federal judge because, when the issue is electrical safety. And most courts wouldn't want to dictate anything to a jurisdiction that they felt could affect safety. It wasn't like the days when we were competing with GE and Westinghouse, two of the largest manufacturers in the country. This was a much larger fight. We were fighting a monopoly.

Little did I think that if I was going to pursue this, I'd be looking at a twenty-year fight with the federal government and maybe some local governments and jurisdictions. "Never enter a fight you don't think you can win" was a sound of piece of street-corner advice that maybe I should have taken. I didn't know anybody who would join with me if I did intend to fight. But I knew a monopoly was wrong, so I continued, but I honestly couldn't visualize a reasonable scenario where I could enter this business. It would take a miracle.

I had to stop dreaming of miracles, get back to reality, and keep running my business. We were still located in a 2,500-square-feet rented facility in Roland Park, a very private residential section of Baltimore that had one small commercial section. The building we were in was a garage, part of a commercial building that couldn't be expanded. We were getting much too big for the space we occupied, and since expansion was part of my business plans, I had to find another space.

After looking in the paper and driving around scouting out buildings, I couldn't seem to find anything that would work for us within my price range. What I did find was a two-acre lot right off a major street. The price was relatively low because the only access to the street was via a driveway about seventy-five feet long and twenty feet wide, but we weren't expecting much outside traffic, so this didn't bother me. I figured that for the money we were talking about, I would still need a mortgage to buy the land and eventually build on it. This also meant I needed Marcia's signature.

Marcia wasn't happy about this.
"Things are going so well for you," she told me. "Why do you need to go into debt with a mortgage?"
"Expansion of the business is not a question. It just has to be, Marcia," I explained.
"Well, I can't say I completely agree, but I won't object to the purchase. I trust you." So although I didn't really have her blessing, I now needed her signature, and I could buy the

property. After about one month, we settled the property. It was just a piece of land with nothing, and I was a man with a vision.

I used all my money to buy the land, so I had to go to the bank to get a mortgage to build the building and finish the site. The bank wanted to see competitive bids, so I put some out the project for open bidding.

I contacted one of the architects I did a lot of work for, Morris Steinhorn. I asked him to design me a fifty-feet-by-one-hundred-feet structure at the far end of the land. This allowed expansion possibilities at the front of the property because I knew I would eventually want a newer building at the front.

Most of the cost in the building was the outside work—clearing the land, connecting the sewer and water lines to the street, and the paving. Of course, I did the electrical design; and Hank Schlinger did the mechanical, which wasn't very complicated.

The interior couldn't have been simpler: just four walls, a ceiling, and a roof. I didn't have an exact layout, so I left it as open as possible. It was split into two halves, each fifty feet by fifty feet. There was a drive-in door in the rear so we could drive a truck in. In the front we constructed two small offices and one big one. This part of the building was air-conditioned. The building was as simple and inexpensive as I could make it, and it still cost a little over $80,000. But the bank was happy to give me a loan for the entire amount.

Our move from Roland Park to the new facility in Patapsco was all done in one day. We drove in a convoy about forty minutes to our new address, 914 West Patapsco Avenue. We assembled the furniture and erected some shelves. Then there was a place to put everything we'd brought—or most everything. A lot still wound up on the floor, but by the end of the day, we were completely moved and ready to do business the next morning.

The building had gone up without a hitch, the move was quick and painless, and before we had time to settle down, business poured in. We got tremendous use out of the facility: storing, repairing, building test equipment, writing test reports, and other administrative functions. My larger vision was to be able to do in-house testing as well and eventually have a full-service test laboratory. I was constantly on the lookout for opportunities to provide some testing in our facility. At least now I had a building where this could happen.

One of the first services we developed in our new building was testing protective equipment like rubber gloves, rubber blankets that were used by linemen when working on energized overhead lines. I constructed a section in our building where we could apply high-voltage to the rubber protective equipment and ensure that there were no pinholes or other openings that would pose a serious danger to persons using them. For my testing business, this was a start, but it wasn't at the level I wanted to have in the building. I wanted the testing we did in our building to be considered laboratory testing. I wanted an entire sprawling gorgeous test laboratory, but I had to wait a few years to get there. And I wasn't patient.

CHAPTER NINE

It was 1970 when Congress created the Occupational Safety and Health Administration (OSHA). Congress stated that their purpose was "to ensure that every man and woman in the nation had safe and healthy working conditions." OSHA assumed jurisdiction over the nation's workplace from states and localities. This new agency claimed jurisdiction everywhere there was an employee-employer relationship.

For the first two years, OSHA wrote lots of regulations involving work safety and work practices. People working in shipyards, for example, needed to wear hard hats and things like that. There was nothing really significant or applicable to my business. I knew that they would have to eventually develop a regulation involving electrical safety. Since federal authority generally supersedes local authority, this type of regulation would affect everyone and every jurisdiction. I reasoned that this was the miracle I needed.

I hoped that any regulation that was developed by OSHA would mandate that each municipality would be required to recognize those that OSHA recognized. Sometime when a federal proposes a regulation that may be in conflict with a state, the regulation would say that the regulation in the state may remain in effect if the state regulation is at least as strict as the federal regulation. In these instances, it could be a matter of interpretations. That would not be a good thing.

It wasn't long before OSHA published a set of regulations, identified as 1910.308(d), stating, in part, that electrical equipment can be "accepted or certified or listed or labeled or otherwise determined to be safe by a nationally recognized testing laboratory, such as, but not limited to, Underwriters Laboratories and Factory Mutual Research Corporation." I was anxious to get to the next ACIL meeting to hear them discuss this provision. It appeared to me that this was the perfect rule to use to open the product certification business to competition. Now, rather than needing to prove we were competent enough to perform this certification to thousands of municipalities, we only had to prove this to one: OSHA.

Or so we thought.

At the meeting, the ACIL attorney said that he'd read the regulation.
"It looks like a good regulation, but it's not the only one," he said. "OSHA needs to write a rule based on this regulation and then needs a procedure to accredit labs."
"How long do you think that would take?" I asked.

"We shouldn't think it will happen fast. From the time a new regulation is promulgated to its implementation could be a very long time."

It was now 1972.

This wasn't really bad news for me. At least there was a way to eventually open the testing to competition, and when it happened, I'd be right there to be one of the first competitors of UL. We couldn't have wished for a better solution. But as many things go with the government, it wasn't a slam dunk.

The first step was to get recognized by OSHA as a "nationally recognized testing laboratory." But they had no procedure in place to accredit anyone. "Gosh, this will probably take two or three years," I thought. Little did I know that it would turn out to be closer to twenty years.

When a regulation is passed in an agency, a department in that agency has to develop a procedure to implement that regulation. Until this is done, nothing happens. I regularly walked through the Department of Labor building trying to see if I could find a way to motivate someone at OSHA to develop the requirement to accredit labs.

"We can't focus on that at the moment. There are more pressing issues at hand," I would hear. Or "let me refer you to so-and-so who is not in the office today. Come back another time to talk to him."

There were other independent labs out there, and I thought surely they had the same frustrations. I talked to the labs that were members of ACIL. They told me they'd written letters to OSHA or a congressman or someone else in power. But I could never find anyone who'd received a letter or was responsible for working on anything related to the rule.

Meanwhile, I still had my other business to handle, and so I put the pursuit of a requirement from OSHA on the back burner for a while. We were very busy, and most of what we did required a lot of my time. Much of our business was with the federal government, which required me to spend a lot of time in Washington. I never went to Washington without including a trip to the Department of Labor building.

I couldn't find any person or department that would be involved with this new regulation. There was no department where this fit. I was passed from one office to another. I really got to know my way around the building. I'm sure in some offices I became a pest, but I didn't care.

Finally, they assigned this program over to the "Office of Variances." I moved fast, now that there was an office and a person to talk to. His name was James Concannon, director of variances. He was a very pleasant person, about fifty years old, and a real bureaucrat.

"I'll be honest with you, Len. I'm not sure how to proceed," he said to me. "I'm looking for guidance on the matter, and frankly, I'm not getting much help."

"Well, it certainly doesn't seem like it's being treated as something that needs to be done," I replied. I knew that if I wasn't there pushing on a regular basis, it would just die a natural death.

"I'm sorry," he said regretfully, "there were just too few people that care about this issue. Plus, there's lots of opposition within and outside the government to accrediting 'for profit' laboratories."

It was discouraging, but it wouldn't by any means be the last they hear from me.

I armed myself with literature about UL and walked around the building, showing the UL logo to everyone I could. The logo showed that UL was a "not for profit" organization, not a nonprofit one. This was very confusing to some. Even one of the solicitors hadn't known this. UL clearly stated in their literature that "they were for public safety and not for profit." I heard at ACIL that UL had lobbied Congress for this addition to the IRS code and got it.

Finally in 1974, OSHA announced in a federal register notice their intentions to develop a program to accredit labs. There were over 130 comments in response to this notice. Most were negative. Comments like "For-profit labs would fudge results to approve unsafe products to please their clients." When something new is proposed and comments are received, every comment must be answered. This is what the Office of Variances was required to do. Mr. Concannon was required to address each comment, and neither he nor anyone else in his department was equipped or knowledgeable enough to do it.

So I visited the office again.

"These comments are ludicrous," I said. "We are honest people who are devoted to the service we provide."

"I understand, Len," said Mr. Concannon. "And we will be discussing the program with legal."

"I know you're saying this to appease me. But this is my career, and we've worked hard to establish the integrity of the industry."

"Here's what you can do," he suggested. "Prepare an application for recognition in accordance with the new regulation. And we'll take it from there."

I knew this wasn't how it worked in Washington, but I was grasping at straws. When the government needs an application to be prepared for any purpose *they* develop the application, they don't ask the applicant to develop it. But Mr. Concannon asked me to prepare an application, and I wasn't to going to tell Mr. Concannon that drafting an application should be the job of the government.

So in March1975 I did prepare an application. I hadn't had any guidance in doing so, so I just starting writing and included everything I thought was pertinent. I'd had some experience with NETA in accrediting field testing organizations. Most government agencies, such as the Federal Trade Commission or the National Institute of Standards and Technology (NIST) that needed to accredited labs, developed the requirements on their own. There were plenty of examples out there to model an application after, but for some reason, OSHA found this task too difficult to do and seemed to keep looking for someone to assign the job to. Though it seemed like it was a waste of time, I had to do it. I wasn't going to give anyone any excuse.

I hand delivered the application to Mr. Concannon personally to be sure he received it. Then the delays and inaction began. His staff was groping for how to proceed. As is typical in Washington, many regulations are promulgated without any direction on how to proceed. I thought this was the job of government lawyers. I think the experience I had with NETA was more experience than the governments had, or maybe I should say that OSHA had. The application I prepared stalled at OSHA for over six months without being read.

While all this was going on, we won a bid to do testing for products at the Mine Safety Company in Pittsburgh. The work involved testing electrical devices used in coal mines to be sure they were safe for use. It was a real laboratory testing project in my new lab; I was thrilled!

Here, safety meant that any electrical device needed to be intrinsically safe. Since a coal mine is an explosive atmosphere, every electrical device used in a mine needed to assure it could not develop an arc that could cause an explosion. We tested products to ensure that a malfunction of the device couldn't result in an ignition or spark that might cause an explosion, a highly critical test that we developed the expertise to perform. The engineer overseeing our work was Ken Klause with the Department of Labor out of Triadelphia, West Virginia. He knew many of the people in Washington and became involved with the new OSHA program because he was familiar with the Mine Safety and Health Administration (MSHA) and knew a great deal about testing laboratories in general.

One day, during a break from the job, I started telling him of my frustration in dealing with Washington.

"I just can't seem to get anywhere," I said.

"You know what I've learned, Len?"

"What's that?"

He looked at me with sincerity. "Sometimes the only way to get things done and move the government is to sue."

"You know, Ken, you're not the only one who's told me this; but coming from you, it really means something."

"That's my honest advice."

I had my concerns. "But don't you think that a lawsuit would only create enemies? I just worry that it would put me at a severe disadvantage if I ever become accredited." Even though

I was getting nowhere in Washington with the people I'd met at OSHA, we had a very friendly relationship. At least on the surface, face-to-face. I assumed that a suit would change that. "If you keep doing what you're doing, nothing will change. A lawsuit gets attention, Len."

"You're right," I conceded. "But I've never sued anyone, and I've never been sued either. My relationship with all the people at OSHA is going to change once I sue them."

"Yes, it will. But think about this: what is keeping the program from moving forward is not the people you're dealing with; it's the ones much higher up, the ones that don't know you and don't give a damn about your issue."

He was so right. It made so much sense to me now, and with that realization, I said, "Ok, that does it. I'm going to sue!"

I discussed the issue with our controller at the company and with members of ACIL to get their opinion as well. We tossed around the idea of trying to get a politician interested in the issue and use his or her influence to motivate OSHA, but I was at a loss as to how to do this. The one thing I did know was that getting any action on this regulation was well above my capability and of anyone I knew.

I didn't know anyone who had sued the government but was once told that if you sue and win you don't really ever win. The government had a way of dragging out decisions and orders. Very often they wore down the opposition with delays and costly maneuvers.

These stories scared me, but they didn't discourage me; it had been over eight years since the regulation had been promulgated, and still nothing had happened. If I stepped back and did nothing, everything would just die. Underwriters Laboratories would go on as before, continuing to exercise their monopoly and charge whatever they wanted. And many new innovative products wouldn't reach the market because manufacturers are hesitated to submit their new products for testing. This would be especially true if no standard existed for the product due to the high costs and effort it took to bring a product to market.

One could say that it was selfishness on my part to pursue this standard; it would bring me a lot of additional business. But the result of a new rule would also open the business to other qualified labs, not just MET. It wasn't selfish. It was principle. It was the fact that for years I was told I couldn't do something I was capable of. I was convinced to continue.

I approached my attorney and good friend Melvin Weinstock about suing OSHA. He was very familiar with filing lawsuits, but they were generally against people who didn't pay their bills or against an insurance company. I don't think he'd filed many lawsuits against the government.

I told him about my experiences trying to get OSHA to do something to act on my application. "Someone I know there told me that the only way to get OSHA to do anything, especially something they don't want to do, is to sue," I told him. "This isn't something I want to do, especially since, if we sued and won, they'll be the ones to review us and can make it really hard for me. So how can we sue and not have them get mad at us?" I asked.

"Here's what I'll do. I'll write them a letter and threaten to sue. Hopefully that will shake them up, and you'll get what you need after only one letter or one trip to Washington."

So we sent a letter, and I followed up with one of the solicitors, so I know it was received.

After an ACIL meeting, one of the very active members—an owner of a chemical lab in Bethesda, Maryland—asked me to have a coffee with him. We walked down to a small café on K Street where he told me he'd been following my experiences in attempting to compete with UL.

He said, "Did you ever consider talking to a lobbyist? Lobbyists aren't politicians. Their business is to persuade or influence politicians. They cause laws to be written and laws to be ignored."

"I hadn't considered that. I was just doing the work myself," I replied.

"Well, you often can't just walk into a politician's office and ask for a favor or to help with a piece of legislation. But a lobbyist can. For all you know, UL has a full-time lobbyist or an entire firm working to block everything you're doing; and if this is the case, you're at an even bigger disadvantage."

This seemed like great advice. "So how do I get in touch with a lobbyist?"

"I have a friend who's a lobbyist. I can get you in touch with him."

"That would be great! Do you have an idea how much it costs to get a lobbyist on my side?"

"I don't. But I do know he lives in a large house and apparently does very well."

"So it's going to cost a lot," I said.

"I think it's your only option," he said. Then he gave me the names of some firms. "Here, I suggest you go visit some of these firms here in Washington and get the information you need. I'm rooting for you, Len."

"Thanks for the coffee and the advice. I really appreciate it."

After our meeting, I walked back to my car, and I realized that I was standing right on K Street, and most of the firms we'd talked about were located within three blocks of where I was.

The miracle I'd hoped for came, but I needed to take action. That's what I was working for. It was no longer totally impossible—it was just nearly impossible. I imagine if UL was hoping for a miracle, it would be that I would go away. After all, who would continue to fight a giant bureaucracy like OSHA for years, without any political, financial, or legal support? Most people would see that as a fruitless fight, a no-win situation; but if any of them had asked my wife, Marcia, why I continued, she'd have to say, "He won't give up, and he won't go away easily." And I didn't.

CHAPTER TEN

Even with the possible legal battle looming, I didn't stop reaching for something new and difficult. Sometimes not necessary, just desirable.

During my beginning years in business, I was often asked, "What college did you graduate from?"

"I didn't graduate" would always be my answer, and it always bothered me. So I set my sights on becoming a registered professional engineer in the state of Maryland. I felt that would be a much better answer than just "I'm not a graduate."

Fortunately for me, my business was successful and needed less of my time and attention. Being registered as a professional engineer was something I'd been putting off for years, and this seemed like the perfect time.

As part of our services, we provided an analysis of the test results for large electrical installations. We also provided a service called a coordination study. This was an engineering evaluation of protective devices, like fuses and circuit breakers. Although there wasn't a requirement to be a registered engineer when performing these services, I still thought being registered could be used to our advantage.

I also didn't know if OSHA could or would add a requirement that the director of a lab needed to be a professional engineer. Even though no such requirement existed, registration certainly wouldn't hurt the matter. And being prepared for the possibility that a registration would be required, would not hurt.

Registration in any state isn't easy. The requirements are rigorous. If the applicant isn't a college graduate, he or she must prove he or she has twelve years of supervisory, responsible, engineering experience in addition to passing a twelve-hour test on "principles and practices of electrical engineering." The test was an open-book exam, which my friends told me was sometimes harder. The only thing I feared was the actual taking of the test. Back in my school days the experience of taking tests was very stressful; I'd done poorly or failed often.

I knew if I were to pass, I would have to devote all my spare time to this exam. My workload at the office didn't decrease, and now I had books on engineering principles to study, which were new to me. The thought that kept me functioning was that nothing in my business really depended on me getting the registration, so the stakes weren't so high.

If it only required an open-book test to become registered, I'd do it.

On the day of the tests I showed up for the exam with only two books: *Electrical Engineering* by Beeman and *Principles of Electricity* by Eugene Key. I looked around at the other applicants. Many came in dragging duffel bags full of books. Now, I was nervous. I only had two books, and one was a paperback! All I could I think about was that many people take the tests two or even three times before they pass. Knowing this made me wonder if I even had a chance.

If only I'd had a few college courses on math and electrical engineering behind me, I thought. My confidence was dwindling.

During the exam, I kept questioning my answers. Many of the questions appeared too easy, so I read some of them again to make sure they weren't trick questions. I looked around the room and saw others routing through one book after another. I wasn't consulting my books nearly as much and wondered if I was doing something wrong.

The testing started at nine in the morning, and we had to be finished by five. At about two I wrote in my last answer and looked around the room to see most people still working on the test.

Maybe I missed something, I thought. I looked over the test

again and again, and couldn't figure out how I'd completed it so much sooner than everyone else. I didn't believe I was that smart. But I was finished, and after about one additional hour of double-checking everything, I turned in my test.

They told us after completing our test we should hear results in about two to three weeks.

Waiting for the results seemed like forever.

I was writing up a report at the office one day, a few weeks later, when Marcia called, "The envelope from the State Board of Licensing and Registration just arrived. Do you want me to open it?"

I felt nervous, excitement building in my gut. "Yes, yes, open it. What does it say?"

The longest three seconds of my life passed as I heard the crackling of the envelope on the other end of the line.

"You passed," she screamed. "It says, 'Congratulations. You are now a registered professional engineer in the state of Maryland.'"

I was thrilled! At the time of my test, I didn't realize that a lot of the work I did in designing and building test equipment was true engineering. I had the life experience that allowed me to breeze through the exam, which wasn't the typical experience of most beginning engineers, who are generally responsible for designing systems in buildings. By doing both, I realized that my experience in building test equipment utilized more of the basic engineering principles than designing systems.

I now looked for ways to use my new professional registration at MET to our advantage. I talked to a few engineers and asked them if they would specify a requirement that a test report on a new high-voltage installation had to be signed by a registered engineer. They all refused. They knew what I was doing and knew my competitors would cry foul. The competitors were GE and Westinghouse, and they certainly had many professional engineers, or PEs, working for them but not in their service shops where the testing was done.

For a while, I did stamp some test reports with my PE stamp when I signed them, hoping it would give us more credibility. But that didn't happen. It was as if I had a biology degree or was working as a manager in a department store. Nothing which I was involved with had any concern with my accomplishment here. I did hang my license in my office but never signed a letter with "PE" after my name. I put my stamp away in my drawer, and that's where it remains today.

Now that the registration was behind me, I knew I had to get back to work on getting OSHA to act on my application. I had to do something or forget it. And forgetting it, for me, wasn't an option.

CHAPTER ELEVEN

In 1973 OSHA began working on its first rule, Part 1907 Accreditation of Testing Laboratories. All of us at MET were very pleased that a rule was finally going to be issued, and we were anxious to file an application even though there were still many issues that still needed to be addressed. For one, there was no procedure to implement this rule, and OSHA had not yet attempted to address these concerns.

But before we had a chance to file an application, OSHA reversed itself and called for 1907's revocation. The solicitor office at OSHA had seen problems in responding to all of the negative comments and decided to handle most of the comments by simply revoking what they'd written so far and start from scratch on a new rule.

I was beyond surprised since OSHA had been so long in getting anything out of the agency. As far as I knew, I was the only one pushing to get the rule promulgated And I was so far down the on their list of priorities that they took their good old time to get anything done. It was as if all the work they had done up to this point was for nothing. Were they just going to start over again at the beginning? I tried to find out the status of the rule but was told that there were too many problems, and the solicitors office had decided to start over with a fresh look at the regulation and the requirements.

"Do you think this delay is UL's doing?" I mentioned in passing to one of the solicitors with whom I talked freely.

"No, it's not," he said. "All I can say is that they really couldn't address all the comments with the rule due to the way it had originally been drafted."

This did not satisfy me. I still had my suspicions and continued visiting OSHA regularly to check on the status of the rule.

All my visits to the OSHA office were for nothing until they developed a way to implement a procedure to determine how electrical equipment met OSHA safety standards. Although I got to know a lot of engineers at OSHA, I couldn't find out who was working, or would be working, on a procedure. I guessed that an engineer would work on drafting the procedure, and an attorney would draft the rule. There were engineers at OSHA who had the ability to develop a procedure, but after a while I began to wonder if anyone had actually been assigned the task of working on one. It appeared that everyone was working on more pressing issues.

I thought I'd speed the process along by supplying what I

thought was a reasonable procedure. So I drafted up a step-by-step procedure, taking into account my expertise in the field and what I knew about other testing companies, and I delivered them to OSHA.

Knowing that the application I wrote for Mr. Concannon was trashed, I suspect that this procedure I submitted was never read by the right people. I found out later that my suggestions could not have been accepted as I would have been the one directly affected by the rule. Therefore, my input could have been judged completely illegal.

It became evident to me that without some external pressure this rule would just die. It also appeared that the outside pressure had to either be political, from a lobbying organization, or legal action of some kind. It wasn't just going to happen because the people at OSHA felt it was the right thing to do.

Then, out of the blue, OSHA stated in a federal register notice that an advisory committee would be formed to draft a new rule. "This is it," I thought. My hopes lifted again. I stayed in contact with the people I knew at OSHA to find out the progress and status of this group. But after about a year I learned that no such group had ever been formed, and the issue remained dormant at OSHA for about two more years. As far as I knew, I still was the only person pushing to get a rule developed. I felt like I was running on a treadmill—

pushing myself harder and harder, faster and faster—but I always ended up right where I started.

I kept up my regular visits, even got to know a few of the OSHA attorneys who would be working on new rule, if they were ever instructed to do so.

In those days, anyone was free to enter the Department of Labor building on Sixth Street. I walked through and entered almost any office I wanted to. I was rarely stopped. Although everyone was very friendly to me and I believe felt my issue was legitimate, they really didn't want to see me because they knew they couldn't do anything to help. Often, when I walked into someone's office, I could almost hear them thinking, "Oh no, not him again. I hate to keep telling him nothing is happening."

Members of the American Council of Testing Laboratories (ACIL) consisted mostly of independent for-profit testing laboratories. ACIL was active with many government agencies; and often their meetings included government officials, including the Federal Trade Commission, the Federal Communication Commission, Department of Energy, National Institute of Technology and others, but never OSHA. OSHA was often invited but never attended. One of their reasons for not attending was that there was pending legislation or they were too busy. With what? Every other agency that came to the meetings had some legislation pending, and they attended. I still went to most of the ACIL meetings even though they weren't of much help to me in getting OSHA to develop a procedure that would accredit labs and help end the UL monopoly.

At one of the meetings I attended, someone from the Federal Trade Commission came to discuss the issue of unfair competition in the electrical products testing area. He told us that the FTC was looking into the matter and was considering developing a staff report and proposing a rule to try to open an electrical product certification market. He presented MET as one of the examples of a company working to become recognized for testing electrical products.

He cited examples where other jurisdictions, not just OSHA, only recognized UL. In his staff report he referenced the OSHA 1907 rule that had been promulgated but sat at OSHA stagnant, with no movement forward. The report also referenced the 1976 Federal Trade Commission complaint to Dr. Morton Corn, the then–Department of Labor Secretary about OSHA's inaction. Particularly, that not only was their inaction unfair to laboratories, but the condition was also limiting competition among manufacturers on certified electrical products. In his response, Corn had stated that OSHA has no interest in limiting competition and concluded by saying that he was committed to making a thorough study of the problem. But again, nothing happened.

Each time I went to OSHA I was told "someone is working on it" but never got any specifics and could never find out who or what office was working on it. It was a typical pass-the-buck response. I followed the progress of the report as long as there was any hope it might have an effect, but I did not push it enough. My best efforts were not enough to find out any information or keep it active.

I could have asked for a special meeting at ACIL to see if together we could have initiated any action at the FTC. However, I alone did not have enough time, influence, or connections to keep this operation going. It needed some internal influence in OSHA, which I did not have. Eventually, it just died a slow death. I and no one at ACIL could find out why. This was my first experience in dealing with another agency other than OSHA, and it seemed like they all operated the same way. Is this how the entire government works? I didn't think I could look forward to any help. I either had do everything myself or I needed a miracle.

Frustrated and discouraged, I continued to pursue OSHA after these top-agency people filed official complaints and I was told that something would be done. But still nothing happened. The issue and I were ignored for more four years.

When the FTC sends a specific complaint to the head of OSHA and OSHA acknowledges that they recognize a problem and will provide relief from that problem, you would expect that relief to come. I know that the political pressure must have been significant to cause the head of OSHA to ignore a request by the FTC even after promising he'd resolve the problem. I guessed that if UL was paying a lobbyist or a politician to keep this rule from being implemented, they are certainly getting their money's worth.

I discussed this issue many times with others mainly at ACIL meetings.

"If a news reporter wants a good story," I would say, "this would be it. Not just the laboratory accreditation issue but the fact that a government agency could tell another agency it would do something and then either not do it or maybe never have the intention of doing it."

In business this would never fly. If a person or company got the reputation of promising something and not performing, they would, at a minimum, lose the respect of the clients and peers. Being on the receiving end of all these empty promises was very frustrating.

"I'm starting to think a lawsuit is the only way to get anyone to do something," I posed to the members of ACIL meeting. Silence.

Then a colleague said, "I agree that a lawsuit is the only way, but you're thinking about going against the U.S. government! Do you know how crazy that sounds? It would take years to get a decision, not to mention all the money you'd be spending."

Even though they all agreed that the only way to move OSHA was to sue, no one at the meeting was interested in joining me in the suit. None of the labs were primarily electrical, and they enjoyed good business in other areas of testing. We were the only electrical test laboratory that was interested in competing with UL. They were all content to allow UL to run unopposed and operating as it had for years without any restraint.

With all my heart I didn't want to sue, but without more options, I knew I had to. I was really disappointed that I was the only one willing to take the step and sue. I knew that if I won, the others would all be ready to ride my coattails; but if it was going to be done, I had to do it. I finally took the advice of my MSHA friend who said that the only way to get the government to do something they don't want to do is to sue them. So sue I would.

CHAPTER TWELVE

My attorney Melvin Weinstock was a very successful collection attorney. Although I generally read, negotiated, and signed contracts we received, I always brought Melvin in for cases where I needed legal assistance or advice. He had written the threatening letter to OSHA, but aside from that, he rarely got involved with any of my dealings with the government.

Often when we got together, I aired my frustrations about my dealings with OSHA.

He would say, "I'll write one more letter for you. We'll threaten again to sue if they don't follow through and act on the application you submitted."

I knew my application had been trashed or at least lost, but we referred to it as if it was still somewhere at OSHA and under consideration. So he wrote a letter and addressed it to the secretary of labor. In this letter, he spoke more firmly, not using the kind of marshmallow words we used in the past. If we upset a few people there by the strong words and the threat to sue, then good. I was in agreement of the letter. It was the kind of letter any normal person would take notice of immediately, motivating him to take action or at least offer a response.

Apparently OSHA was used to these kinds of threats and completely ignored them. I stopped into their office about a week after they received the letter. The person in the solicitor's office told me that they had received the letter.
"It's being reviewed," she said politely, but they wouldn't offer any kind of comment prior to an official response. An official response never came, or if one was sent it got lost in Melvin's office.

After this letter, my relationship with the people at OSHA changed. I no longer received the warm friendly responses I had in the past. It seemed like I was the enemy, at least to the people in the solicitor's office because they were the ones who needed to respond. I was more confused than ever, with an abundance of options, but none seemed to offer the perfect solution. Was this the time to consider seeing a lobbyist? Or should I stick with Melvin and pursue the lawsuit? How much would it cost? Is it even going to work?

The only person I knew that I could talk to about this was the new executive director of ACIL Joe O'Neill. I planned to stop in the ACIL office the next time I was in Washington to talk to Joe O'Neill. I wanted to see what they had to say about suing OSHA. "I was worried when I heard you wanted to speak with me," he began.

"Worried? About what?"

"I just have a bad feeling that you're thinking about resigning from ACIL."

I almost laughed. "Not at all. I just have a few questions from a business perspective, and I want your two cents."

"About the UL monopoly?"

I nodded. I didn't need to explain my situation to him; he knew it well. "What do you know about the use of lobbyists?" I asked him.

"I know there are a number of them in the building, but I don't know any personally. Why do you ask?"

I said, "I was wondering if it would be a good idea to see if they knew anyone at the Labor Department that could help produce a rule for accrediting labs. The legislation is already there. They don't need to influence legislation. Just make sure the agency does what the legislation requires them to do."

"I see. Well, I'm not sure, but I will try to find out. It seems like a good approach."

Two days later, I got a call from Joe. "I spoke with someone who knows how lobbyists work," he started, "and most of what they do involves interacting with politicians, not an agency head or anyone in the agency. It would be difficult to find a lobbyist who has experience with OSHA or the Department of Labor. You would need someone that has influence there."

"Thanks, Joe. I really appreciate it." I hung up the phone and thought for a while about what he recommended. I took his advice to heart, but in the end I decided not to pursue a lobbyist and stand by Melvin, who was becoming more and more infuriated with the situation.

Four months had gone by with no response to the letter, and Melvin was ready to sue. "I'm not used to this," he exclaimed. "You may not mind being ignored, but I do. Let's get together and file the suit now. No more waiting. They think because you're not a big corporation, they can walk all over you, so let's do it."

The following day, Melvin filed a suit seeking one hundred million dollars in damages to force OSHA to act on my application. The one hundred million was to get their attention, to show them that we were serious, and OSHA probably knew that.

I was absolutely convinced that after the suit was filed, OSHA would wake up and start making some necessary changes. But I was wrong. I was wrong on many issues involving OSHA and what I predicted they would do.

If I would have concentrated half of the time on my business as I had on pursuing OSHA, I would have had more business than I could handle. But this *was* my business and the business I wanted. So I continued, undeterred.

The suit was filed in federal district in September 1982, eight years after it had all started. After filing the suit, I debated with myself about going into the OSHA offices, as I usually did. I held off for about two weeks. But I got anxious, and I couldn't wait any longer so I decided to make a special trip to OSHA's offices. I got in my car and made the one-hour drive from Baltimore to Washington DC. I parked the car at a meter on Sixth Street, just outside the offices, and sat there, arguing with myself about whether to go inside. *Is this a good decision? Will this really change anything? Will anyone even talk to me in there?* After about fifteen minutes of back and forth, I put the keys back in the ignition, started the car, and drove back to my Baltimore office, questions still racing through my mind.

I did feel that the people in the Office of Variances weren't of the same mind as those in the solicitor's office. I believe that if any of them had heard anything from the solicitor's office, they would have told me. But they weren't the decisions makers and their opinions didn't matter.

The next week, I got a call from Melvin.
"OSHA has filed a notice to dismiss," he told me. "This is a common move, and I'll answer it right away with a motion to remove the dismissal order."
He did just that, and it was granted. OSHA now had to file an answer or agree to develop a procedure in accordance with the regulation.

We finally received a court date to present our case. We were scheduled to meet in federal court on April 2, 1983, in front of Judge Andrew Young.

"This is it," I thought. "Finally we're going to receive some response and be on our way to becoming a nationally recognized laboratory."

"If the judge agrees with us," Melvin said, "that would be the end. OSHA will have to agree to accredit us."

"What if they appeal?" I asked.

"Not likely."

The night before our court date was a sleepless one. This would be my first experience in court for anything, much less suing the U.S. government. Suppose the judge actually ordered the government to give me one hundred million dollars. Suppose the whole case is thrown out. Suppose I emerge victorious from this battle.

The next day, as is typical, I showed up at the courthouse an hour early. Melvin didn't show up until ten minutes before the scheduled time. We sat together in the gallery, watching the prior proceedings, until a clerk called the case.

"Wait here," Melvin told me, as he made his way to the front. "I'll let you know if I need you."

With power and confidence, Melvin explained the situation fully. Those representing the government stood there in silence until they were addressed by Judge Young. At that point, they agreed that there was a need to develop a regulation to remove the anticompetitive situation. I observed the proceedings for a short thirty minutes. The exchange was much gentler than I expected. In the end, Judge Young ordered OSHA and Melvin to cooperate in drafting a settlement agreement. They agreed, and that was it. It was over.

I had a meeting in Melvin's office to prepare what I wanted to see in a settlement agreement.

"So let's lay out that the hundred million dollars in damages will be dropped in exchange for a good agreement," Melvin proposed.

"That just doesn't seem fair," I said. "I would like to see some money in the settlement agreement."

"You know we can never win damages on this issue," Melvin replied.

"Well, how much is being screwed around for ten years' worth? How about you ask those guys if they know how much additional money UL has pocketed by not having competition for the past fifteen years!" I was livid, and I rarely raised my voice. But this was the first time I got visibly upset about the situation.

"I understand your frustration, Len, but have to drop the damages if you want to get a settlement." I took a deep breath and calmed myself down. He was right. "So let's talk about what you want in this agreement," he continued, unfazed.

"All I want is for OSHA to be reasonable and fair in

determining our capability." "So should we include accreditation criteria in the agreement then?"

"We don't need to. The criteria already exists for laboratory accreditation but not for electrical products labs specifically. We should tell OSHA to develop a procedure that will use these existing criteria for accreditation."

"And that's all?" he asked.

"That's all. It shouldn't be complicated." There were many agencies accrediting labs, and any of them could either provide OSHA with the procedure they used or would work with OSHA to develop one.

So OSHA, with Melvin's assistance, drafted a settlement agreement dated April 22, 1983. After a few weeks of back-and-forth negotiations, the agreement was approved by all parties, and it seemed like things were finally moving.

In the agreement, OSHA stated that they "believe[d] that it [was] necessary to eliminate the anticompetitive effects unintentionally created by references . . . to UL and FM and by the agency's failure to implement . . .1907." (1907 was the rule OSHA had published in 1973 and revoked one year later.) Further, OSHA professed itself to be "greatly concerned about the special status given to UL and FM."

What a crock, I thought.

To correct the situation, OSHA agreed to develop a rule deleting the terms "Underwriter Laboratories" and "Factory

Mutual (FM)" wherever they appeared in applicable regulations and to "create a workable procedure for the designations of enterprises whose approval of products [would] be acceptable to OSHA."

This was how OSHA stated their reasons for the settlement agreement. They did not say it was the result of their inaction and how they had to be ordered by the court to enter into this agreement. They forgot to mention that this action was a result of being sued and ten years of stonewalling. But they didn't fail to mention how greatly concerned they were about the special status they had given UL.

Once the agreement was finalized, OSHA began the complex process of creating the new regulation. In January of 1984, it published a regulatory analysis in which it admitted that rule 1907 had not been implemented in part because it would have been too expensive.

In this analysis, OSHA conceded that by "requiring that certain equipment be tested [and] certified by a nationally recognized testing laboratory such as Underwriters Laboratories, [or] Factory Mutual Research Corporation," they had "effectively established an OSHA sponsored equipment testing duopoly for UL and FM."

In fact, it was not a duopoly at all but rather a monopoly because consumer electrical products were tested by only UL and non-consumer equipment such as gas and fluid products or mechanical controllers were mostly tested by Factory Mutual (FM). The issue still stated that any electrical- or appliance-type manufacturer who wanted to sell its product in the United States must first get approval from UL. This monopoly would exist until OSHA completed its work to promulgate the requirements and certify labs to provide the testing and certification.

In January of 1984, everything seemed to be proceeding smoothly. Then inexplicably, everything stopped. OSHA had promised to have a new regulation in place on March 9, 1984. That date came and went with no further activity. I couldn't obtain an explanation from anyone. When I did get in touch with persons who normally provided information, I was met with a cold "I don't know" or "Don't ask me."

I had to surmise that some powerful external force had been able to exert pressure to stop this action, an action that had been approved by everyone, including a court of law.

Beyond frustrated, I asked myself what more I could do. Maybe a newspaper reporter could expose what's happening. Maybe Melvin should be more forceful and upset (at this point, his settlement agreement could now be used for toilet paper). I wound up with nothing. OSHA probably figured that I would throw in the towel. Don't get me wrong. I was close, but I wasn't there yet. How could a democratic government just ignore a court order and delay its action with empty words?

I wasn't ready to give up, but I got very busy with my business and was constantly debating with myself about whether or not it was worth the trouble to keep knocking at OSHA's door. This standstill added another four years to the nearly decade-long timeline. Of course, all this time UL was getting bigger, richer, and controlling more of the market.

I was also getting fed up with Melvin. Everyone told me to get rid of Melvin and hire a lawyer that would follow up and stay on top of OSHA and sue them every time they violated an agreement. I knew that if I hired another lawyer, I would have moved faster or even found out who was pulling the strings. I had a strong guess, but it was always a guess and didn't say anything about it to Melvin. In hindsight, I should have hired another lawyer, but I didn't. I always thought it was too late to bring another lawyer into the picture.

I asked Melvin if we could go back to court and ask them to order the government to comply.
"That would be another suit," he said, "and we would need to file again."

That night, when we were getting ready to go to sleep, Marcia sweetly revealed, "I'm worried about you, Len. What if OSHA tries to retaliate?"

Marcia was a great wife and mother, and she was incredibly smart, but she rarely got involved with any of my business decisions.

"They can't, and they won't," I reassured her with no way of knowing whether this was true.

"Well, just be careful. Think about your family."

As I fell asleep that night, I thought about making another trip to the OSHA offices just to check in. After work the next day, I headed straight back to Washington DC to do just that. I talked many of the people in technical support and also stopped by the solicitor's office. They all agreed that they were in favor of my action, and it seemed like there were problems from the front office, although they never actually came out and said it.

After this visit to OSHA, I felt like my mission was reborn, and I was anxious to tell Marcia how the visit went.

"Most of them thanked me for being willing to sue," I explained to her. "They all felt that the inaction at OSHA was driven by politics at the top. All the career employees, the people I speak to on a regular basis, were extremely happy that someone came up to end this unfair bias."

She was very pleased.

Something turned around for me after that; I started receiving praise and support from other labs and especially manufacturers that wanted to get away from UL's grip on the community. It was the general consensus that opening up the certification market was good for everyone. All the people I knew in the testing business said that it took a lot of guts to pursue this case like I did.

Most of my business was testing large electrical systems in the field, and neither OSHA nor UL had the ability to affect me in that arena. My business came mostly from contractors or large building owners such as hospitals or governmental organizations. The laboratory testing business, however, was completely controlled by OSHA and dominated by UL. Manufacturers were thrilled because, if I was successful, it would open up their market. I was now more determined than ever to win for the integrity of the business not just for myself.

Meanwhile, we were still getting some laboratory testing business from mostly small manufacturers who were making one-of-a-kind products for localities where MET was approved by the local jurisdiction. But this couldn't sustain a full-time operation. We always tested to a national standard and needed to continue to prove experience of testing to the national standards if experience would ever be part of the accreditation process. We tried to account for any possibility that could be listed in a recognition requirement by OSHA. I strongly felt that we would have to be flawlessly prepared to prove our capability because the opposing forces were strong.

Although the issue at the court was to have OSHA develop

a laboratory accreditation procedure, it wouldn't specify the requirements; OSHA alone would be doing that. The suit didn't even request or require OSHA to accredit us just to review our application. My mind flooded with all the possibilities.

What if the requirements are so strict that I or anyone else couldn't meet them? Would we have to go back to court and further prolong the process? What if OSHA makes the requirements so strict that accreditation would only come to those with the right connections? What if there are caveats in the regulation that would make it favorable to some and unfair to others? If OSHA could be influenced to stop the implementation of a rule that was promulgated in 1973 for over ten years, what else could that influence accomplish?

And what about UL? Even though the suit didn't involve UL, could they still influence the regulation? If my suit forced OSHA to accredit other labs as equal, what would happen to UL's tax exempt status?

UL was a not-for-profit organization that didn't exist until they lobbied Congress to create it. At the time, they stated that their purpose was to provide for public safety, not to make a profit. If they kept their status, they would have an unfair advantage. Test equipment was our biggest capital expense; when we bought new equipment, we paid a tax. UL didn't. UL had a lot to lose if and when the rule was final and other companies could compete with UL on an equal basis. I don't know why I had to be concerned for UL in this area.

They had been operating like Jesse James without a gun for over fifty years, charging what they wanted, only accepting products they wanted, and having inspection authorities around the country enabling them.

So many questions had yet to be answered, and no one could foresee where the case would go, giving me an awful lot to think about.

CHAPTER THIRTEEN

The field testing business was booming at all locations, which meant I was extremely busy. I didn't have any help with the technical issues facing us, and that is what took up most of my time outside of the office. This was good for two reasons: it kept money flowing so I was able to pay my bills, and it kept my mind off the suit. Although, I later wondered it that was a good thing.

One of the things I had to do in the office was look over invoices and ok them for payment, plus I was the only one who signed checks. Tillie was our bookkeeper who had been with me for over twenty years, but she was getting older and didn't want the added job of checking an invoice without me looking at it first. My accountant had been after me to hire a person who could do more than Tillie was able to do, but I just did not know how to let Tillie go. She was with me for a long time, and I had lots of trouble finding the words to tell her that she was no longer needed.

Nervously, I called her into my office one day and said, "Tillie, I think you can see the business is getting a lot more involved and beyond what you have been able to do. I have been losing sleep because I did not want to hurt you, and I thought letting you go would be a major hurt for you and me."

"Lenny," she said calmly, "I don't want you to feel the least bit hurt. I have been thinking about retiring for a long time. I'm getting too old to wake up early in the morning and be here by 8:00 a.m. You are doing me a big favor. Like you not wanting to hurt me, I didn't want to hurt you by telling you I would be leaving. Now we are both happy, and no one is hurt."

I was relieved and a little bit sad. It would be hard to see a loyal employee go, but with Tillie leaving, I was now free to interview and hire a person that could do her job plus help with other office and business issues and to digitize our accounting system.

I put an ad in the *Baltimore Sun* classified for a comptroller. It stated, "Medium-sized company in need of a comptroller with computer skills."

I received lots of résumés, but I picked out one that especially impressed me, someone that was just starting in the computer age. His name was John Steven. I brought him in for an interview.

"Tell me about your previous employment, John," I said.

"I worked in the accounting department at my previous

job and excelled there. I made all their records completely digital, and now I'm looking for more challenge and more responsibilities."

His explanation had me feeling comfortable about his abilities, and my gut told me to go with him. My gut was right; he worked out perfectly, quickly moving our accounting department into the computer age. This simplified the process to determine our true cost of a job and if we were making money on some of our projects.

More than that, he was able to understand my business and issues with OSHA. It felt good having someone at the company I could discuss business issues with, including my issue with OSHA. I enlisted John's help in reading contracts and purchase orders I received as he would pick up on important things that I'd missed. There were other things I wanted to accomplish, such as moving into the laboratory testing business, though all the delays at OSHA had were still stalled. We were also outgrowing our building and needed to expand. I had the land to build on but needed time to hire an architect, obtain financing, and so on. John stepped in to take some of the load off my shoulders.

I was lax in not continuing to pursue OSHA after they'd agreed to a settlement and then pulled back. But I was extremely busy. We had offices all over the country, and there was certain engineering work only I could do. I wondered during these times if the people at OSHA were ecstatic when I didn't come back after they openly violated a court agreement. I pictured them sitting in a conference room discussing the suit and saying, "I guess we got rid of him," bursting into fits of laughter.

When I attended the ACIL meetings with other testing labs, they'd always ask me if anything was happening. I believe they were all under the impression that things were proceeding no matter how slow. The only thing that kept me from actually ending my push was the fact that I couldn't sit back while UL was taking advantage of the American system and getting richer doing it. I still had business with Melvin, and he'd ask to me if I wanted to sue again. I never gave a straight answer because, in all honesty, I didn't know what I wanted to do.

I confided in my new employee John Stevens. One day, he said that pursuing the lawsuit and spending a lot of time and money might not be a good idea because it was taking my time and attention away from the business.

"Since UL is so entrenched," he said, "even if we did get the recognition, could we get the business from UL?"

It was a lot to consider. It felt good to have these discussions with someone in the office. Marcia wasn't easy to discuss these business issues with. She made the issues seem so simple that I had trouble talking to her about them, so I didn't. She used to say, "Just do this" or "Just do that," but nothing was simple in my mind, so I just dealt with the issues in my way.

One day, out of the blue, John said, "Len, don't take this the wrong way, but if you're going to pursue OSHA again, I think you ought to consider another lawyer. A big firm but not the biggest. Just one that has the experience and reputation in suing the government. Just like in your work, you know that there are companies that know how to do things much better than others. I think that if OSHA was being pursued by a larger law firm, they would have a different attitude."

I'd never thought of this, but after a while, I did agree that John was right. The problem was that Melvin worked with me, and even though things were now good, a large law firm would probably want a large retainer. I could have found the money I needed for a larger firm, but I didn't pursue it. This was my biggest mistake. I assumed that if I had a board of directors, they would not have let me find all of these excuses for not moving forward faster. If I had factored in all the costs—trips to Washington, fees to Melvin, and the money I was losing by not getting the business earlier—it would have more than covered the costs. But I didn't, and this caused me to lose a few more valuable years.

CHAPTER FOURTEEN

In the nonpolitical world, failure to comply with a court order resulted in some very stiff fines or even jail time. Evidently, that's not the case with government. In 1984, when a court ordered the breakup of AT&T, they complied, leading to a major restructuring. AT&T was a national company with widespread influence. At that time, Western Electric Company was a division of AT&T and the sole manufacturer of telephones and telephone equipment in the United States. It was the Federal Trade Commission (FTC) that identified them as a monopoly, took AT&T to court, and won the suit, opening up the telephone business to competition.

It was the responsibility of the FTC to identify monopolies and end them to ensure there is always free and fair trade in the United States. Since Western Electric Company was the only company that manufactured the equipment and AT&T was the only buyer, it was determined to be a monopoly.

The court-ordered breakup required AT&T to divest itself from manufacturing telephone equipment and allow other equipment to be connected to the telephone network, provided this new equipment met AT&T standards. These requirements were developed to prevent any damage to the fragile telephone network. Suddenly, other manufacturers of telephone equipment began to emerge, eager to enter this huge market. They quickly manufactured telephones and telephone equipment and had to prove that this equipment met the new requirements.

In no time at all, the Federal Communication Commission promulgated certain regulations that all new telephone equipment had to comply with. It didn't take them years or even months to develop the requirements; it was all done relatively fast in order to satisfy the court. The regulation that resulted was entitled part 68, title 47 of the Code of Federal Regulations. Its purpose was "to provide for uniform standards for the protection of the telephone network from harms caused by connections of terminal equipment thereto."

The purpose of the FCC rules was to protect the telephone network from harm, not the consumer. The requirements in the FCC rules part 68 listed specific test requirements that had to be met for a device to be legally capable of being connected to the telephone network and not causing damage to the network

New telephone manufacturers, anxious to enter this new market, solicited independent labs for this testing work, and of course we bid on the projects. This was my first real opportunity to set up and provide laboratory testing services that wasn't in UL's realm of services. So I immediately jumped in to provide this testing. We became one of the first labs in this business.

At the time, we were in the process of altering our five-thousand-square-feet building to become our official telecom Laboratory. But the new lab in the building would not have been completed fast enough to meet the swelling demand for testing, so we began by conducting the testing in a converted house trailer on our property.

The opportunity in the telephone industry was not only good for us and other testing companies but for manufacturers as well. Electronic manufacturers from the United States, China, Korea, and other countries immediately jumped on this huge market, designing and producing the most high-tech and fanciest phones they could (had this monopoly never been broken, we may still have a black phone with a rotary dial on our desk and at home). But the phones had to function properly and comply with industry regulations. Making the phones was not difficult; making them comply was something they had never faced before.

As one of the first labs to provide compliance-testing services to telephone manufacturers, we had no trouble finding customers to use our lab for the part 68 certification. The procedures to provide this testing were fairly simple: we just had to furnish the FCC with our test procedures and our capabilities. The National Institute of Standards and Technologies (NIST) established the National Voluntary Laboratory Accreditation Program (NVLAP), and we obtained their accreditation to provide part 68 certification, greatly enhancing our credibility and establishing our capability with the FCC.

Unlike OSHA, the FCC didn't take years to develop a procedure for doing this work, and NVLAP didn't take years to develop criteria to accredit labs. The new standards and accreditation were all completed in a matter of a few months. I was finally in an area of laboratory testing that wasn't controlled by UL's dominance.

I felt proud to be accepted based on our capability as engineers, particularly since we'd never tested telephones or telephone equipment before. We had excellent engineers and the ability to obtain the equipment to demonstrate it to NVLAP, the agency that accredited us to do this work. There were no politics involved in accepting MET to perform these tests; the process was seamless.

There were many other areas in field testing where I was able to expand, but that's not where I wanted the company to ultimately go.

North of us was a field testing company called Burlington

Testing Company in Burlington, New Jersey. They had started to do what I was doing by quoting firm on projects, and they were becoming successful. But they were struggling. Due to bad management, they were pretty deep in debt and headed for bankruptcy. I knew the president from my involvement with NETA, Dick Beach, and talked to him frequently.

"We're having union problems," he explained. "The union is making us operate as an electrical contractor."

It was the electrician union that controlled his hiring and men. That was a killer for this kind of business, and even though I was also union, I had negotiated a separate agreement that allowed us to do our own hiring and work men all hours outside of regular hours.

So when Dick approached me in mid-1985 about buying Burlington Testing Company, I jumped at the opportunity. This purchase brought on a slew of new clients from that area and eliminated a huge competitor for me in the electrical testing market. I also acquired a lot of new employees, and I needed them because my government clients were growing.

I had to convert Burlington Testing Company to the MET way of doing business and treating customers. Naturally, this took a lot of my time, and I couldn't do the follow-up I need to do to keep after OSHA. I brought Burlington's technicians to Baltimore for training. I also made many trips to Burlington to oversee their operations and make sure the acquisition was going smoothly. When trying to resolve the union issues, I came across many problems, and this took a lot of my time as well. There always seemed to be something that happened that took my time and kept me from pursuing OSHA.

One important source of business for us was the *Commerce Business Daily*. It is a government publication. I read this paper like many people read the daily newspaper. This paper advertises all government procurement and contracts to be bid on, including other government advertisements. I was always looking for opportunities with the government, and this paper is where I found those opportunities. One day I saw a notice that The Mine Safety and Health Administration (MSHA) was considering contracting out some testing services. Often the government places a notice in the *Commerce Business Daily* when something is first being considered. That way they hope to hear objections before they proceed on something. I investigated this as a good possibility for laboratory testing we could get into. The work would be awarded by MSHA out of their offices in Triadelphia, West Virginia. It's just one-hour drive from my office in Pittsburgh, and I felt I needed to personally drive out there and get in on the ground floor of the project. A winning proposal would grant us this project, and I felt we were in a prime position to obtain the contract.

When the solicitation came out, we wrote a long proposal describing our capabilities and interest in obtaining the contact. And we heard back shortly after submitting the proposal that we won. This was another kind of testing that we had never done before. We were assigned to test electrical devices used in a coal mine, an atmosphere that is highly explosive due to the coal dust. The testing assured that if a failure occurred, such as a small arc in an electrical device, the failure wouldn't result in an explosion. We tested this equipment for manufacturers in addition to MSHA. We tested all types of devices to be safe for use in the explosive atmosphere of a coal mine.

Oddly enough, the Mine Safety and Health Administration (MSHA) was a division of the Department of Labor, a sister to OSHA. At MSHA we were able to test and certify critical devices that, if not exactly in compliance to the standard, might result in a major explosion with serious repercussions. The stakes were very high for the work we were doing with MSHA. But OSHA didn't feel we were competent to test home appliances or computers. What really bothered me was the fact that some people at OSHA evidently thought the engineers at UL were more competent than our engineers.

We were very busy, and I had too many other pressing problems at the time to try to get OSHA to proceed as they'd promised. But I couldn't let it go too long or it would just die. I had a meeting with my attorney, Melvin Weinstock, which resulted in him writing another threatening letter to OSHA, but as the other letters went, it was ignored. I wasn't blessed with any political help. I didn't have any business friends with whom I could discuss this issue. I didn't have the connections that would help propel my case forward. I had to do it on my own.

I discussed the OSHA issue with John Stevens, my new comptroller. I showed him all the correspondence with OSHA and explained the lack of response from them. I tried to give him some of the details on the issues I had been dealing with.

"I know enough about government procedures and their policies," he said, "to say that I'd be willing to bet that someone is trying to keep you out just as hard as you are trying to get in."

"It certainly feels that way," I replied.

He shook his head. "This is a tough fight, and I'll do what I can to be more than just your comptroller but your right hand. It would really help if you knew who it was pulling the strings. We both know that if strings are being pulled, UL is behind it, but the question is who in the government is doing the pulling?"

"I've thought about this for a long time, and I've come up empty-handed," I explained. "I don't know who in the government is actually responsible for this, and I don't know how to find out." I felt like I kept rehashing these frustrations over and over again, this time with John, but it didn't make things any better. It just felt good to have someone to talk to.

My best advice still came from Melvin Weinstock, whose

advice was to sue again. If I hadn't been as busy as I was with my other work, I wouldn't have hesitated. The first suit had taken a lot of my time and money, and I really didn't have either to spare. I was working five days a week, from 6:00 a.m. to 6:00 p.m., and Saturday or Sunday usually found me at the office as well. Due to the nature of our work, we often had jobs during the weekends and I often showed up with the men

Every time I was in Washington, I continued to stop by OSHA's offices to see if there was any progress or if I could do anything to move it along. As a member of the American Council of Independent Laboratories (ACIL), I had occasionally attended their government affairs committee meetings, and I was always asked for a status on what was happening at OSHA. My answer was always the same: "I don't know."

I knew there was political pressure on the top people at OSHA, most likely from a Chicago senator or a connected congressman, but I couldn't prove it. Even if I had proof that this was the case, what would I do with that information? Being a paid member of a national association in Washington, I should be entitled to use their resources to find something out. When I asked about it at the last meeting, I was told they did not know and would explore to see if they could find out anything. I was not happy with their response, but I did feel if they could help me they certainly would. It seemed like they should not consider it for me personally but for the testing business as a whole. But they did not reflect that was their position, which was upsetting to me. Still, I waited to find out what they could do.

It should have been obvious to me that I was getting nowhere at OSHA. I needed higher level of involvement at OSHA, and if I did not get it, nothing was going to happen. With all I have been through, I should have understood that continuing the way I was, was not working. But since my business was going well, it became less and less of a priority.

CHAPTER FIFTEEN

I waited three more years for OSHA to comply with the court order, and they didn't. I knew I had legal recourse here, but I let it go thinking it was futile. Either OSHA or UL or both were wearing me down, and it was working. I was really disgusted with OSHA and didn't know if another court order would change anything. It appeared that OSHA could do what it wanted, and my choices were to give up or go back to court. Would it be any different if I won again? I made an appointment with Melvin in his office. We sat down, and I asked him what our next steps were.

"You have three choices now," he said, "whereas before you only had two. You can go back to court and sue again, you can forget it, or you can meet the top guy, the secretary of labor, and threaten him with exposing his agency to the news media."
"How would I do that, and would he care?"
"Tell him, tell his assistant, tell anybody below him that you will contact the media. You will explain that they succumbed to political pressure to ignore a court order in favor of a not for profit and it's hurting a small business."

"But how could I say he is bending to political pressure? I don't know that."

"It doesn't matter if it's true or not or if you can prove it or not. It's just that we throw it out there and hope it sticks. Try to get public opinion on your side."

I was apprehensive. And Melvin could read it all over my face.

"But if you can think of something else," he continued, "let's do it."

"I'm stuck. I guess we have no other choice. Giving up is not an option," I told him. "Well, let's see what we can do with him. Before the secretary of labor wouldn't meet us, but now I'm sure he will."

So the appointment was made. Melvin called the attorney we dealt with during the negotiations and said he wanted an appointment or we would be back in court the next day. We got the appointment with assistant secretary of labor John Henshaw.

I picked up Melvin from his house in Baltimore, and on the way there we talked about many things not related to OSHA or MET, including the idea of working with a bigger law firm. It had been a nagging thought for a while, and I was curious what he thought.

"Melvin, do you think that if I hired a high-power law firm, we could accomplish our objective?"

"How so?"

"Well, many of these big law firms have attorneys that came

out of government. They know the government inside and out. Could that be what it takes? Could they look at you as an ambulance-chasing attorney and figure that they can steamroll you? Because, in all honesty, it looks like that's what they are doing." I knew deep down that Melvin was the wrong person to ask this question. Of course he would say it was not necessary, but I asked anyway. I was setting him up to the possibility that I might hire another lawyer if this didn't work, and although I knew I should have been more concerned about me and not Melvin, but that is the way I am.

"If that's what you want, we can do it. I do know some big firms in Washington and can ask them to work with me in the next suit, and the government will see them associated with the case. I don't know if that will change anything except what it will cost you. But we can't just try it. If I get someone else involved in the case, though, they need to be involved. I can't get them to add their name to the suit and just be silent."

"Do you think we're going to get anywhere with him today?" I asked.

"I don't know, but the fear of going back to court made him grant us this appointment. It's anybody's guess what will happen. But there's a fifty-fifty chance he'll instruct his staff to move on your application. You're not asking anything unreasonable, just to act on your application."

We arrived and found our way to the office on the second

floor. It was an impressive executive suite, lavishly outfitted with thick carpet and beautiful mahogany furniture. We were greeted by the receptionist and asked to wait.

We sat there for about ten minutes when another lady, perhaps his secretary, came out and said, "Mr. Frier, Mr. Weinstock, I'm very sorry but the secretary was called to the White House on urgent business, so he has arranged for his assistant Mr. Wright to see you. Please follow me."
Under my breath I said, "Bullshit, White House." But being brushed off was nothing new to me, and I wasn't going to leave.

"Secretary Henshaw sincerely apologizes, but he cannot refuse to attend a meeting at the White House when requested," Mr. Wright explained regretfully. "I know the entire story with MET and getting 1907 implemented, so let me do what I can to tell you where we are."

"I don't care where you are," Melvin blurted out. "I want to know when this regulation will be implemented so Mr. Frier will not be blowing in the wind, like he has been for the past eight years. You agreed to a date when the regulation would be final. That date was over three years ago. What would happen to an employer if he let an agreed-upon date with OSHA to go three years delinquent? I want to know when OSHA is going to abide by the settlement agreement. And if you can't give us that date, I'll be back in court and ask the court to give me a date."

I was nervous. I wasn't one to be aggressively confrontational, and I hadn't expected this kind of rant from Melvin. But I didn't stop it. It pleased me that he was airing our frustrations. Melvin continued, "And I'll also ask the judge to order the secretary himself to be part of that agreement and personally have him appear in court. Because you have so flagrantly ignored the previous court order, I think I can get the judge to provide that order. Now I want to know when you'll give me a firm date and when OSHA will have the regulation completed."

Mr. Wright was clearly shocked by Melvin's rant and said, "I can't give that date because I don't know it, and neither does the Secretary, but I'll convey the message."

"I'm tired of dealing with messengers," Melvin fumed. "Make sure you convey it accurately. Also tell him I'm sorry I didn't meet him today, but if we don't get satisfaction in the next few days, we'll be back in U.S. district court in Baltimore very shortly and can meet there." Melvin turned to me and said, "Let's go, Len."

We walked out of the office down the long hallway in silence. I was shocked.

When we were well away from an earshot of the secretary's office, I said to Melvin, "Do you think it was smart beating on him like that? You know you really pissed him off, and he's just a flunky. I hope it was smart; I'm worried."

"Don't worry," he replied, "I wanted him to know that we won't be easily brushed aside any longer. We now have the upper hand because they've violated a court-agreed settlement. Judges don't like that, and we should take full advantage of it."

On the drive back to Baltimore, we didn't talk much about OSHA, although I tried to get Melvin's thoughts on what OSHA would do next. He said that if we didn't hear back from them in two days, the next move wouldn't be theirs—it would be ours.

And that's just what happened. Two days came and went, and we didn't hear back. I was completely flabbergasted by the arrogance. These guys got appointed to a high position and must have felt that they were king. Even when a court ordered them to do something, they ignored it. I didn't think that could happen. I was hoping that when we did go back to court, the judge would order the secretary to be in court for failing to abide by the settlement agreement they had initially agreed to.

It didn't take more than one day to prepare the suit and file it. Melvin asked for an expedited review, which was granted. The suit was filed, and lucky for us, it was assigned the same judge, Judge Joseph Young. At our hearing in front of Judge Young, it was obvious to me—and I'm sure to the OSHA attorney Mr. Bernstein—that Judge Young was angry. He read the case and actually showed how surprised he was that this action was still not resolved.

The first issue was that the government moved to dismiss the suit. Below is a transcript of the proceedings:

THE COURT: *I am sure OSHA would take the next five years, given the chance to do so, to litigate this case. They are not going to do it in my court anyhow. I'm really a bit irritated at [OSHA's] position in this case of first having been dragging their feet in 1982, then having agreed to a settlement 1983, having delayed it until 1984, and here we are in 1987, almost 1988, and they have done nothing about it. They will get no consideration out of this court as far as I am concerned.*

MR. BERNSTEIN: *Well, with all due respect to the court, I can't say [OSHA] has done absolutely nothing during this time period. There are priorities—*
THE COURT: *It hasn't been resolved the issues that were required to be resolved by the [settlement agreement].*

MR. BERNSTEIN: *That's correct. And the court's original response was [OSHA's] done nothing. And the fact is, [OSHA] has done something and has attempted to promulgate this standard.*

Your Honor, keep in mind that what OSHA has to do is promulgate standards to protect workers in the workplace. There are other issues that need to be resolved that, with all due respect to [MET], are a little more important than protecting some competitive interest in the community.

THE COURT: *I understand that, but then why not resolve these issues? Why keep [MET] hanging, twisting in the wind for—well, actually it goes back to 1974. Doesn't there have to come to an end to this with OSHA's doing something to resolve the issue?*

MR. BERNSTEIN: *Absolutely, Your Honor.*

THE COURT: *Well, where are the equities in this case?*

MR. BERNSTEIN: *Well, Your Honor, the equities in the case are that [MET] is entitled to allow [it] to attempt to be accredited in order to approve the electrical equipment.*

THE COURT: *And when are they entitled to it? After they go out of business because they have not been able to do it? I am simply criticizing [OSHA] for taking every step they can to thwart the implementation of an agreement they agreed upon five, three, four years ago. As far as I am concerned, they have no equities in this case.*

MR. BERNSTEIN: *I'm sorry, Judge.*

THE COURT: *They have no equities in this case. The continuing process of foot dragging has to stop, and if anybody has to stop it, I'll be willing to do it.*

Then after a brief conference, the government lawyers apparently got the message and offered a new agreement that a regulation would be promulgated within 120 days. Then Mr. Bernstein did something remarkable. He indicated to the court that his client OSHA might continue to drag its feet if it saw any way to get around the court's new order.

MR. BERNSTEIN: *Your Honor, I've just been told that the [court's new] order should state specifically that the rule-making process must be completed in 120 days.*

THE COURT: *That's all I'm saying.*

MR. BERNSTEIN: *No, it's a language problem. Counsel advised me we'll have a much easier time in getting our client [OSHA] to complete it within the scheduled time period if, number one, it's an order and, number two, the rule-making process must be completed.*

THE COURT: *The order would say the defendant be and hereby is ordered to complete the rule-making process within 120 days.*

I sat in the on the side as this was all going on, regretting that we hadn't brought the action long ago. Melvin didn't need to do much talking; the judge was doing all the talking. I was glad that we got Judge Young because I think, with another judge; Melvin's arguments wouldn't have been as successful.

"I'm a little upset you didn't push me to do this sooner," I told Melvin after the proceedings had concluded. "I hadn't seen the injustice that OSHA was doing to me as clearly as I should have."

"Well, better now than never. Let's make sure it sticks this time," he said.

This time, without any wiggle room, OSHA complied. On April 12, 1988, it promulgated its new rule for the recognition of nationally recognized testing laboratories. Of course it did give UL an additional ten years to exercise their monopoly and expand their business without lifting a finger. The new rule was identified as 1910.7 Nationally Recognized Testing Laboratories. It specified that third party (or independent) testing for safety would be necessary in order for certain equipment and materials to be deemed acceptable for workplace use, with testing having to be performed "in duly accredited laboratories."

The new rule set out four "specific and exacting" requirements that every nationally recognized testing laboratory (NRTL) had to meet, and NRTL would be the designation used to accredit a lab. Even UL would have to use this designation. First, a lab had to be capable of performing the required testing. NRTLs were expected to do their testing in-house. Subcontracting or performing tests outside the laboratory were only allowed in the case of "unique or special needs." Second, a control procedure had to be implemented for the listing or labeling of products, including production line inspection during manufacture. The third requirement called for organizational independence. The requirement for independent or third-party testing had always been a requirement of code enforcement agencies for fire and electrical safety testing. Finally, the NRTL needed to develop an appeals procedure.

None of these requirements were difficult for MET to implement; we already had most of them in effect. We'd been accredited by NIST and accepted by a number of cities for the field labeling of products. Many of these requirements were what OSHA will be asking for. And if we didn't have it in place to OSHA's satisfaction, it would be easy to add or modify what we had because we were so small. We were ready to go.

We didn't need to advertise that the regulation was fully adapted. We were in most of the business papers around the country like the *Wall Street Journal*, the *New York Times*, and the *Chicago Tribune*. The *Baltimore Sun* sent a reporter to interview me. I received many phone calls from people I didn't know congratulating me. The calls were mostly from manufacturers who told me to contact them as soon as we felt our recognition would be equal to UL's. I wrote down a lot of names and put them aside. They said things to me like "UL needs competition" and "It's about time. They had their way too long."

It seemed like we were over the wall of impossibilities and could now be accredited as equal to ULand we should also be as acceptable.. We had just received what we should have had ten years prior. Because of all the stonewalling and behind-the-scenes manipulating, we had to wait ten years and finally sue three times to get justice. This had been one hell of a wall to climb, much more difficult than I ever could have imagined. Had I known back then what it would take to reach this point, I never would have attempted it. Little did I guess that my real challenge had only just begun.

I thought I'd be receiving calls from manufacturers ready to send me their products. I was a little naive in thinking that all the jurisdictions through the country would just back off now that we were officially approved and the court had spoken. It was sort of a shock to find out that none of the jurisdictions cared if OSHA would approve us, and they were the final authority in approving a lab.

I never referred to the names I wrote down or called anyone back as potential customers. I needed to be sure that all of our testing would be acceptable everywhere. I still had a few more walls to climb. Walls that a court or judge couldn't get me over!

CHAPTER SIXTEEN

I realized that to take full advantage of our new recognition as an NRTL, I'd have to start concentrating on the laboratory product safety testing business, which would mean delegating some of my field testing duties to someone else. In the past, I struggled with delegation; I would take on most of the tasks myself. And it was the one of reasons that I took over fifteen years to get this far. The field testing was the bread and butter of the company and kept me solvent for our entire existence, and although it was running smoothly, it still needed constant attention. If I was going to concentrate on developing the laboratory testing part of my business, I would need to continue making a profit with the field testing. That was my sole support. So I either had to hire someone to develop the laboratory business or promote someone in the field testing section to take over for me. Field testing or laboratory testing—where did I want my business to go?

My accounting firm at the time was Ernst & Young, and lucky for me, I had a smart and savvy account manager named Bruce. I told him of my dilemma to move forward with the laboratory business and that I needed to make a decision.

Bruce understood the business and felt my best opportunity was to explore and develop the laboratory testing business.

"You have to jump forward with both feet," he encouraged, "and it would probably be in your best interests to sell the field testing business. That will give you the freedom and time to pursue the laboratory business and the money you need to really develop the laboratory business."

This was something I hadn't considered. "It won't be easy to find a buyer," I told him. "The most logical ones would be electrical contractors. I'm sure many of them would have the money and interest, but most of our clients would be other contractors, their competitors, so they won't get the business."

"It doesn't have to be someone already in the business," Bruce said. "Others may be interested."

"Who would be interested in purchasing a field testing business?" I asked.

"Perhaps someone who just has money and wants a going business that's already developed. Ernst & Young is a very large firm, and we have contacts with people in these positions. As a matter of fact, I personally know someone who might be interested. He could buy the business outright or buy in with an option to take control, or you could arrange some other option."

Of course I was interested. It all sounded good, and at the time, I didn't see any downside except to lose control of the field testing operation. I asked Bruce, "How does this get started? What do I have to do? Will you become an agent or what?"

"I can't be an agent," he replied, "because both parties are my clients, but I can talk to this person and explain the business and see if he's interested. If so, then I'll arrange for you to meet."

Bruce called me two days later to say his contact was interested. I was really surprised it happened so fast. An initial meeting was arranged at my office a few days later. If the sale worked, it would solve a lot of my problems in growing the laboratory business.

I called Melvin to tell him what was going on. If there was to be a deal, I'd need Melvin involved. I told him all I knew and promised I wouldn't make any commitments until he was on board.

At the appointed hour, Bruce and his client showed up at my door. The man's name was John, and he looked like he had just stepped out of a fashion magazine. He was tall and poised, very well dressed in an expensive designer suit, silk shirt, and French monogrammed cuffs secured with shiny gold cuff links. He was a very good-looking professional gentleman, about sixty years old. I was surprised that someone dressed like that would visit anyone in South Baltimore, much less my little blue-collar business. If it was to impress me, well, it worked. I sure was impressed but didn't necessarily see him as a fit to buy MET; he just didn't look the part.

I almost blurted out, "I think there's been a mistake," but I didn't; and instead I gave him a tour of the building, showing him everything he wanted to see. There wasn't much to the tour: just the offices, some of the test equipment we had in building, a few trucks, some job sheets, and a partial list of customers. I tried to explain the business as best I could to someone I knew had no knowledge of a large electrical system. He asked a lot of good questions and left after about forty minutes. I was sure that would be the last I would see of him.

I was shocked again, when Bruce called me early the next morning and told me John was interested and wanted to see more. He mainly liked the idea that we had very few competitors. Actually within a two-hundred-mile radius, we had none. GE and Westinghouse had, for the most part, removed themselves from the testing business.

So John came into the office early one morning planning to stay most of the day and observe a typical day of operation. He wandered the premises, talking with employees, and learning the ropes. Around noon, we went out to lunch and talked about what I saw as the future for this side of the business.

"There's definitely a bright future for field testing," I explained to him.

"I can see that," he said. "And after spending most of the day with you, I feel comfortable being able to run the company."

"What about the day-to-day operations? No offense, but you

are not an engineer and it can get very technical."

"Oh, I don't think there will be a problem with that. I plan on either hiring a technical person or promoting someone in the company to handle those issues. I feel that the most difficult part of the business is the managerial end, and I have the ability to do that."

We briefly talked about the price of the company and how it would be paid. We tentatively agreed on a procedure and that we would get Bruce, our accountant, to develop a value.

We agreed that John would buy in with a minority interest and the option to take complete control of the field testing business, although he thought that the laboratory testing division was the best company to own because it was a more professional type of company, my desire was for him to take over MET Testing, the field testing group, not the proposed laboratory testing division. And I was sure to make that very clear.

As my new partner, John relieved me of many of my responsibilities. He stepped into the roles that he could do well, like hiring new employees. I used to spend maybe fifteen minutes in an interview and make up my mind immediately. He'd interview for over an hour and then need additional time to be sure.

He hired an electrical superintendent named Bill from one of the large contractors in Baltimore. Bill was on top of everything in no time and turned out to be a great employee. But even with John's help, I still didn't have all the time I needed to develop the laboratory.

And in addition, there was something about John that just didn't sit well with me. He didn't have a very friendly personality and turned lots of people off with his superior type of attitude, something I hadn't seen when we first met. He wanted the office area to be an executive suite for him and an administrative assistant that he'd brought with him, not an open space to everyone in the company. He kept throwing accolades at me to impress me; and I didn't realize it at the time, but he was quickly moving toward owning the entire company, not just the field testing division.

One day John stopped me in the hallway. "Len," he said with a sly smirk on his face, "I've got some news for you."

We stepped to one side as I asked, "What news?"

"I just hired an electrical engineer," he said.

"Good, tell me something about him."

"He's a graduate electrical engineer from Bucknell University. I had him in my office for over an hour questioning him. He starts next week."

"Is that all you can tell me about him?" I asked.

"No." He paused, still smirking. "It's your son, Robert."

After hearing this, I could have dropped to the floor. Robert is my youngest child, my only son, and I always had hopes of him taking over my company. I have two older girls. The oldest, Cheryl, attended the University of Maryland and graduated with a degree in early childhood development. My middle daughter, Susan, also went to the University of Maryland and graduated with a nursing degree.

Neither of my daughters' educations had prepared them to take over running MET, and they didn't ever appear the least bit interested. So you can imagine how happy I was when my son majored in electrical engineering and went Bucknell University. I often dropped hints that MET was a wonderful company, a place to thrive and grow, but Rob had other plans after he graduated college.

Almost immediately after graduating, Robert went to Israel to work on a kibbutz. He planned to make aliyah (a Jewish return to the Holy Land for citizenship) and become an Israeli citizen. Working for MET didn't seem to be part of his future plans.

After living in Israel for four years, he decided to return to Baltimore, where he briefly worked for MET. I don't think he enjoyed it very much, and I partially blame myself. I was very used to giving orders and would rarely solicit other opinions or points of view. Although we never fought or argued, Robert decided to leave MET and start his own business. He went back to college, receiving an MBA from the University of Baltimore. Then, he founded a small business but didn't see a future there either. Robert has always been incredibly bright, the kind of person that needs to be his own boss, and he needed something that would challenge him and make him happy at the same time.

I often felt tension between Robert and me, and because we never really sat down and talked about any problems he felt existed between us, I didn't recognize that there was a problem. This tension was not due to a lack of love. I love him with all my heart as much as I love my other children. When I look back, I admit I may have pushed Robert too hard to work for MET. I couldn't help it; he was an ideal employee for the company: logical, hardworking, independent, and extremely intelligent with a warm sense of humor.

When Robert decided he wanted to work for MET, he approached John instead of me. My heart sank when I realized this; I felt ashamed that my own son didn't feel comfortable asking me for a job. But at the same time I was ecstatic that he had brought in the best employee to make MET a success. .

The deal that Bruce had helped broker with John sounded good to me on the surface; it would free up my time to focus on the lab testing business. But I quickly learned that, in a business deal, if you don't know who you're dealing with, you better have a good lawyer. Well, as it turns out, I didn't know who I was dealing with and didn't have a good lawyer who could spot what was happening. Melvin was good with collecting bills and suing insurance companies, but he was no match for my new partner and his lawyers. John's lawyer had drawn up the contract, and Melvin had looked it over.

The contract stated that John was to work with me as a vice president. I was to handle all technical and customer-related matters. He was to deal with the men and the union and handle all financial matters. His objective was for us to start making money. He felt the company was hemorrhaging money because I wasn't watching the finances closely enough, and that was true. My biggest concern was building a strong reputation and broadening our abilities as a field testing company, not making money.

This contract looked fine to me; I would get some much-needed cash and have time to expand the laboratory testing business. But as time went on, John tended to change things his way, even though he didn't know anything about the business. I didn't notice the changes immediately, but Robert did, and it bothered him. John's manner of giving orders to employees was intimidating. They all rejected his attitude and policies, causing a lot of tension within the ranks.

Robert approached me one day, looking concerned. "John is planning to take over the company," he said.
"I know, Robert. The contract allows him to buy a majority of the field testing business."
"Not just the field testing business," he said.

My ears perked up. "What do you mean?"

"I mean, I looked over the contract, and the way it's worded, he has the ability to get a majority interest in *everything*, field testing and the lab. And he's working on doing just that."

I was shocked but not all that surprised. I had had a bad feeling about him from the beginning.

"We needed another lawyer to look at the contract," he insisted. "I'll send it to a friend of mine who works for one the top law firms in Baltimore, Gordon Feinblat."

This firm, actually one of Roberts friends, read the contracts and immediately saw the deception that was cleverly worded into the contract. A deception that Melvin didn't see. The new lawyer set up a meeting with Robert and me and decided the best thing to do was to write a letter to John and tell him that his tactic wouldn't work, that John would never obtain a majority interest in the company; he would always be a minority stockholder.

The day after John received the letter, he came into my office, fuming. "What is this? You can't break this contract. It's in writing, in black-and-white. You try to break it, I'll sue you for everything you have!"

He was a vicious man, and I knew he would do anything he could to hurt me and not lose his position.

To be honest, I was scared. I called my new lawyer and told him what John had said. He told me not to worry, that John's behavior was to be expected from a person like him. However I was worried because I knew how John could be very vicious I know John probably had a very good lawyer, but fortunately, I had a much better one We set up negotiations to restore the company back to me. The deal was to have a board of directors meeting and fire John, an option available to me under the contract. Then the fight began.

The negotiations weren't pleasant. John made things difficult, even for his own lawyers. It was so bad that the lawyers on their side had to meet in different rooms and go back and forth. It got to a point that we threatened to hire a litigator and have a judge decide a how to settle the issue. I just wanted him out. The final result was that he bought the field testing portion of the company and I kept the laboratory. As soon as it was his, he sold the operation to a very large electrical contractor, making all the employees very happy.

When I look back now, I was more than pleased that John, as cunning as he was, decided to pursue MET because I didn't recognize then that Robert would turn out to be the best thing that could have happened to MET or to me. By Robert joining the company when he did, he was able to recognize that which I couldn't see, and he saved the company. I was so lucky to have my son on my side. Often things unexpectedly happened to me that worked in my favor. I'm sure John thought he was so smart in hiring Robert and thumbing his nose at me. However, the time came for him to regret it.

Over my career, one opportunity had followed another, and only good things had resulted. I'm not that smart on these matters, but I believe it was some kind of divine intervention that saved me and the company.

CHAPTER SEVENTEEN

Now that a rule was finally promulgated and the procedures were written, we needed to undergo an audit of our laboratory by OSHA and prove that we were capable of testing products to the applicable standards. Only after a successful audit could we be recognized as a nationally recognized testing laboratory (NRTL). This meant that we could legally certify certain electrical products and our certification would be acceptable everywhere in the United States (as we thought at the time).

Our new problem—and an even higher wall to climb—was that, in addition to obtaining business from manufacturers, we had to be able to compete with UL. After all the years that UL had maintained their unfair advantage because of OSHA's inaction, they were granted full acceptance as an NRTL with no audit. To UL's benefit yet again, OSHA adopted the following provision in the appendix in its new rule: "Notwithstanding all the other requirements and provision of 1910.7 and this appendix, [Underwriters Laboratories and Factory Mutual Research Corporation] are recognized temporarily as a nationally recognized testing laboratory." I knew that they had to accept UL without any break in their acceptance since UL approves hundreds of products a week. But I thought it was unfair to me, but it had to be.

We were definitely at a disadvantage in attempting to compete with UL even after we were officially accredited. The government's deliberate delay of our recognition or that of any other laboratory gave UL years to further establish themselves as the only lab that could certify electrical products. We knew that UL wouldn't be an easy competitor. In addition to all their obvious advantages, they had instant name recognition and were accepted without question everywhere. Almost all the safety standards used in the certification process were written by UL in committees chaired by UL representatives. Included on these committees were many of the major manufacturers, electrical inspectors, and other regulators. It gave UL a major advantage when their personnel rubbed elbows with people in the industry.

Ask any card player if he'd play cards when the deck was stacked in his opponent's favor. This was the game we had been fighting for years to enter and now we were in it, so we were going to play.

We still had concerns. How could UL be granted temporary recognition when they hadn't been subjected to any type of audit, particularly since all the requirements were unknown until a final rule was promulgated? UL had been operating in a state of rule less limbo for many years, with no incentive to maintain any of their facilities or equipment since they didn't have to report to anyone. To counter this argument, UL filed an affidavit stating that it had operated within OSHA regulations, leaving it up to MET to prove otherwise, although we never claimed UL hadn't. We attempted to obtain documents relating to OSHA's inspection of UL, but the government initially refused to release them, claiming "deliberative process privilege."

One of these privileged documents turned out to be a memo from lead auditor Kenneth Klouse to OSHA in which Mr. Klouse stated that following a review of UL's Client Test Data Program (CTDP), Compliance Management and Product Assurance Program (COMPASS), and Total Certification Program (TCP), he was forced to conclude that UL operates organizational programs that appear to not be in accordance with the scope of the interpretations used in evaluating an NRTL's capabilities. This deviation would require review by OSHA legal personnel. Though the government was insisting that UL wouldn't dare operate outside OSHA rules, OSHA's lead auditor, Mr. Klouse, had documented something very different.

In announcing its decision, the court reiterated its authority to enforce the settlement agreements, notwithstanding the variable classifications of 1910.7 as a "regulation." The court ordered OSHA to expeditiously complete its review of UL's and FM's applications. This created a problem for OSHA since its own audits had established that many of UL's programs, affecting billions of dollars' worth of commerce, might not meet OSHA's rules. Shutting down UL was hardly an option, and there was no proof that any of the noncompliance items discovered during the audit would result in the endangering of the health of either the workers or the public. For the government, the answer was easy: if UL couldn't comply with the rules, just change the rules.

But that wasn't as easy as it sounded. To make these changes, they had to implement the Administrative Procedure Act, which required a complicated rule-making process that often took years to complete and years was longer than Judge Young would be willing to wait.

Fortunately, someone at OSHA must have seen this one coming; five months before the court's decision, the agency put one of its best solicitors, Dan Jacoby, on the case. Jacoby had interviewed various parties at OSHA and felt he could prepare an interpretation that would expand the rule's envelope to encompass what UL was already doing. In other words, they would just change the rules.

It frustrated me that, to accommodate UL, the government was willing to bend over backward while MET barely got a wink and a nudge. But this was typical, and by this point, we were used to it.

That new interpretation was released about a month after the entry of the court's order. In it, OSHA cited the four elements that defined an NRTL. The first was "the capability to test and evaluate equipment." OSHA explained that, although the capacity existed, it didn't mean it had to be used in all cases. The next requirement stated, "As long as an NRTL, which is not economically affiliated with a manufacturer, had the ultimate authority and responsibility for approval . . . the needs of independence would be satisfied." Under this condition, the independence requirement would be satisfied. OSHA further defined the scope of what an NRTL could do. They could, but were not required to, accept data from other NRTLs and, under specified circumstances, could sign off on testing data and product evaluations supplied by other entities.

Now the way was clear for OSHA to accredit us. By this time it had been over sixteen years since I filed my first application to become an NRTL and compete in the laboratory testing business. The U.S. government had put into place a procedure that allowed not only MET to become accredited but also any other test laboratories that felt they could qualify according to the rules.

The basis of my suit had always been for OSHA to act on

my application and determine if we met all the technical and administrative requirements, not to automatically accredit us. The requirements hadn't existed until I sued. At this point the government had to rush a procedure to audit us. The rule should have been written years ago but waited until they were under a court order to get it done. So the next step was to be audited by some of the people that had been fighting me for almost twenty years. If successful, MET would legally be allowed to test, certify, and label products for use in the home and workplace.

The procedures to be used in my audit had not been officially established. But OSHA was forced to proceed with what they had without delay. I imagined the many impossible requirements the audit could create. What if they asked us to show experience in testing and certifying certain products when we were not legally able to test these types of products? This would put us at their mercy, with my only recourse to go back to court and cry foul. That could add another year or two to the process.

Needless to say, I didn't have a good feeling about the audit. I believed they felt they were taking a risk in accrediting me due to our lack of experience. They never called me in advance to tell me who the audit team would be or what would be included in the audit. So I had to wait until they walked into my lab to find out. The day before the audit, at 5:00 p.m., I had a meeting in the lab with all those that would be involved with the audit. I ordered some pizza's, and we all sat around, trying to anticipate what questions they may pose.

Sue Sherman—one of the attorneys from OSHA, whom I did speak with on occasion—told me, "We have to be confident that no one can believe that an outcome of the suit is that you won accreditation without being qualified. We have to be absolutely sure that once you gain recognition you meet the strictest standards." From this I had to assume they would be trying to turn over every rock they could find to look for something.

I told this to the team, "How could we know what to expect? We all agreed we had to be sharp and be ready for anything." After going over everything we could think of, I told everyone to go home and have a good night's sleep. "We're as ready as we'll ever be. Tomorrow is the day."

CHAPTER EIGHTEEN

At 9:00 a.m., on April 22, 1989, six representatives from OSHA arrived at the MET laboratory: two attorneys, two people from technical support, and two engineers from MSHA. The only ones who had experience with a lab, as far as I knew, were the engineers; and one of them was Ken Klause, whom I got to know during the testing project we had with MSHA. Even though Ken was my friend in a professional way, he was still very focused on the audit. Most of the time he answered questions the others had relating to something we were doing or not doing and served as a source of expertise for the group. I guess I was fortunate that Ken was one of the team since he knew laboratory testing issues.

After they arrived and were seated, Sue Sherman, the team leader, explained some rules to us, "You are not allowed to provide coffee or donuts to the group without them paying the actual costs. No matter how trivial, you must avoid the appearance of favoritism." Whenever we had important visitors or customers visit us, we always stocked the conference room with coffee and donuts; it was an unwritten rule in the business world. Whenever I visited a company, coffee and some kind of snack always seem to be there. I found it offensive and frankly ludicrous that they thought I would be able to buy influence or a favorable assessment with a cup of coffee. But I abided. I put a jar next to the coffee pot, and they paid me fifty cents for each cup of coffee.

After they finished the rules on coffee and lunches, we entered a pre-assessment meeting. Sue Sherman introduced everyone from OSHA, I did the same for my staff, and then we began the audit. I was a little worried because our company had never been analyzed like this before. Our conference room wasn't comfortable for six people, and there were no convenient restaurants nearby, so we had to order in lunches from a nearby restaurant and ate in our conference room.

They carefully scrutinized our equipment and calibration reports. Most of the time they looked at our equipment; they didn't always seem to know what they were looking at. There are hundreds of standards on electrical products that we would eventually need to prove we had the capability to test. But at this initial stage we only needed to prove we had the ability to test to a few, about fifteen. They went through every item in each of the standards and required us to show that we had the capability to do the testing. If this was to be our test, I knew we would have no problems. All the OSHA people must have felt a tremendous amount of pressure to perform a quality audit that could withstand the most objective review, and I could sense it.

At first I didn't understand what the attorneys were going to do, but then it became evident that they needed to prove that we were completely independent of any outside supplier or producer of any products we may certify. They went through our financial information to prove our independence. They went through all our purchase orders from the previous three years, looking for any clients that could potentially be a supplier to us. Fortunately we did not buy many supplies and there were very few purchase orders.

The audit lasted three full excruciating days. Except for some small noncompliance issues that could be easily corrected, nothing was found that could hold up the accreditation, and we were pleased to find out that we passed! Of course the court ruling required that the final report first be submitted to OSHA headquarters or the office of the secretary before the report was official. But I knew MET would receive accreditation. I was told I'd be hearing back shortly, and MET was considered to have complied with all the requirements.

As a by-product of the court ruling, the implementation of the regulation would also allow other labs to submit applications to become accredited. Now that our audit was complete, we were the first nationally recognized testing laboratory in the United States, paving the path for most other electrical product testing laboratories follow in our wake. In fact, I received calls from many of these labs thanking me for my efforts. I'm sure their applications were all filled out and ready to be submitted, right behind us.

After the excitement from the audit died down, I sat in my office and reflected on what it took to get me here. I thought of the time Hank Schlinger told me I had a high wall to climb to compete with GE and Westinghouse. I knew I had to call Hank to tell him that that wall was nothing compared to the wall I had just finished climbing.

Finally, on May 16, 1989, after more than sixteen years, I was invited to attend a signing ceremony at the Department of Labor building. Here I would receive my official certificate and recognition as a nationally recognized testing laboratory, an NRTL. I brought my son Robert, our sales manager at that time, and Cecilia Lobe, my director of marketing. The number on my official certificate was 1.

I thought I might have the signing with the secretary of labor or at least the assistant secretary of labor, but neither showed up or made a statement of absence. The representative from OSHA assigned to the signing was the assistant to the assistant, Allan C. McMillan; he signed the certificate. I'm sure some bad feelings remained from our previous visit to the secretary's office where Melvin had told them off. But we bore them no ill will but I did not venture a guess on what they thought of us. It was over!

Every once in a while, when we received a large testing contract or completed a very large project, I would pop open a bottle of Asti Spumante, and we would have a little toast to celebrate. But for some reason, I didn't feel like celebrating after the signing. The realization of what was still required to be successful was starting to sink in. Getting the recognition had clouded my vision on what lay ahead. Now that I had the accreditation, I couldn't enjoy it as I thought I would. I looked into the future and thought, *Is that it?*

In order to turn the laboratory testing business into a profitable venture, I needed clients—lots of them—and this could be my hardest climb yet. All I had so far was the ability to legally do the testing and certifications. I needed the electrical inspection authorities in every jurisdiction in the United States to also accept MET, and there were over ten thousand of them! I needed the manufacturers to give us the work and the consumers to accept the product with the MET label in an industry where, for the past eighty years, all they had known was UL. Without all that, I had nothing, just a piece of paper to hang on the wall.

All manufacturers who make electrical or electronic products for distribution in the United States want their products universally accepted. If a jurisdiction—any jurisdiction—

refused to accept the MET mark that would restrict where a product could be sold, and no manufacturer would accept that.

Most of the business we obtained in the past was from smaller manufacturers of commercial or medical products that were not for universal distribution but rather geared toward a specific jurisdiction. We were also contacted by manufacturers who were frustrated with UL for various reasons. They contacted us thinking we could do something UL would not do. Most of the time they were disappointed with our answers. One of their first questions was if we were accepted in a particular jurisdiction; this was our biggest disadvantage. This required us to approach the jurisdiction and find out if they would accept the MET mark. It seemed we were constantly convincing an authority somewhere to accept the MET mark. If they wanted any supplemental information, we provided it. If they wanted to visit our laboratory, we not only allowed it but paid the inspector's transportation and expenses. This was handled on a case-by-case basis. But to sell products in large retailers, like Home Depot or Lowe's, manufacturers needed approval in all ten thousand jurisdictions. How could I even contact all of them? If I couldn't find a solution to this, the piece of paper hanging on my wall would mean nothing but sixteen years of fruitless efforts.

I had no idea what to do, but I was not going to give up.

The Washington Post

Washington Business

APRIL 18, 1988

OSHA Regulation Opens the Door For Electrical Testing Companies

By Warren Brown
Washington Post Staff Writer

BALTIMORE

Deliverance came in Vol. 53, No. 70 of the Federal Register, dated Tuesday, April 12, 1988.

The section affecting MET Electrical Testing Co. Inc. ran 23 pages—consuming dozens of columns and requiring tens of thousands of words, much of it written in small, annotative print.

It meant that the Baltimore-based company had won a 15-year battle against the Occupational Safety and Health Administration, a victory that could radically change the industry that tests and certifies the safety of electrical equipment for industrial and commercial use in the United States.

The ruling in the Federal Register, effective June 13, breaks the longtime dominance of the testing industry held by Underwriters Laboratories Inc. and opens the business to greater competition and controversy.

Opponents of the rule contend that the regulation could cause a proliferation of unscrupulous product testing and certification services—organizations that would fudge figures and findings to get more profits and clients.

Indeed, the regulation could affect the way

estimated $1.2 billion business occupied by nearly 2,000 companies, most of them small and obscure.

As a group, those labs have tremendous power. Their product standards and certifications affect the costs, quality, safety and availability of nearly all items sold in America.

MET, with $8 million in annual revenue, is a relatively small player in the electrical testing and certification field. Since 1894, that business has been dominated by Underwriters Laboratories, a nonprofit safety testing and certification company founded in Chicago and now headquartered in Northbrook, Ill.

UL practically started the electrical standards and certification industry in the United States. Its round labels of certification are found on millions of products—everything from toasters to gargantuan generators used to supply power to communities nationwide.

The UL presence is so overwhelming, its labels so ubiquitous, that the company often is regarded as a governmental agency. Therein lies the rub, as MET saw it.

Local, state and, until 1973, federal agencies frequently required UL certification of electrical products sold within their jurisdictions. Electrical equipment used or installed within factories, cafeterias and government offices, as well as electrical components in gov-

Baltimore-based MET Electrical Testing hopes its recent victory will help it to expand its business.

tions responsible for a large part of the privately developed product standards in the United States.

For a variety of reasons, OSHA never implemented the 1973 rule. The agency never defined "nationally recognized testing laboratory" either.

Instead, from the viewpoint of the smaller labs, OSHA made things worse by using UL and FMRC as examples of "nationally recognized" labs. In the absence of a clear definition, potential customers misconstrued the examples to mean that UL and FMRC were the government's preferred testing laboratories, critics said.

"OSHA created a monopoly," said MET

Small, lesser-known companies like MET complained that the governments had given UL a monopoly by mandating its services in a market occupied by equally qualified competitors.

In 1973, the federal government yielded—somewhat. That year, OSHA, which monitors work place safety, published regulations designed to admit more companies into the business of safety testing and certification of electrical and other products used in federally regulated industries.

The OSHA rule called for testing to be done by "nationally recognized testing laboratories ... such as, but not limited to, Underwriters Laboratories and Factory Mutual Research Corporation."

TYPICAL OF THE NEWS PAPER ARTICLES AS THEY APPEARED THROUGH THE US

U.S. Department of Labor   Occupational Safety and Health Administration
Washington, D.C. 20210

May 24, 1989

Reply to the Attention of:

Mr. Leonard Frier
President
MET Electrical Testing Company, Inc.
916 West Patapsco Avenue
Baltimore, Maryland 21230

Dear Mr. Frier:

I am pleased to inform you that, subject to the conditions and
requirements of 29 CFR 1910.7, as of May 16, 1989, MET
Electrical Testing Company, Inc., has been recognized as a
Nationally Recognized Testing Laboratory by the Occupational
Safety and Health Administration.

This recognition is limited to equipment or materials which,
under 29 CFR Part 1910, require testing, listing, labeling,
approval, acceptance, or certification by a Nationally
Recognized Testing Laboratory. This recognition is limited to
the use of the following test standards for the testing and
certification of equipment or materials included within the
scope of these standards, listed by MET product catagories.

This accreditation will be valid for a period of five years
from the effective date of May 16, 1989, until May 16, 1994,
unless terminated prior to that date.

Sincerely,

Alan C. McMillan
Acting Assistant Secretary

LEONARD FRIER AND ALAN McMILLAN AFTER THE SIGNING CERMONY AT OSHA

Occupational Safety and Health Administration
Nationally Recognized Testing Laboratory Program

NRTLP

Certificate of Recognition

MET Laboratories, Inc.
914 West Patapsco Avenue
Baltimore, MD 21230

is recognized by the Occupational Safety and Health Administration (OSHA) as meeting the requirements for a Nationally Recognized Testing Laboratory (NRTL) established under Section 1910.7 of *Title 29, Code of Federal Regulations*. This recognition is limited to testing and certification only within the current scope of recognition and is subject to all other terms set forth in the letter of recognition and in applicable *Federal Register* notices. This recognition continues in force beyond the "*Effective through*" date below provided the NRTL has filed a timely request for renewal with OSHA. For current recognition status and other recognition information, contact the OSHA NRTL Program or visit *www.osha.gov*.

John L. Henshaw
Assistant Secretary of Labor
Occupational Safety and Health Administration

May 23, 2007

Effective through

1

Certificate No.

CHAPTER NINETEEN

Following the incident with my former business partner John, I realized I was spending too much time worrying about competing with UL. This was a distraction and took my efforts away from where I needed to focus. But now that we had won the suit, I wanted to start directing my attention to the market for new customers and building our lab business.

John, my controller questioned why I was fighting such an uphill battle to get the product safety certification business off the ground. The telephone testing business was steady and profitable, and there were more customers to pursue in that sector. We were also developing the capability for testing products to various environmental conditions such as: temperature extremes, vibrations, even simulated earthquakes. To test this equipment, there were no requirements for approval from a local jurisdiction, To perform these tests, we built various test chambers to put devices into and installed the equipment to assure that the devices being tested meet the requirements in the test.. To acquire a customer for this service, we didn't need to get everyone around the country to accept us; we only had to convince one client and his customer that we were capable of doing the tests. Usually the customer was the U.S. government or a major defense contractor. And our business expanded from there. So why was I fighting so hard for the lab business? It didn't make sense to Marcia and even made me question it myself.

I thought long and hard about this. And I concluded that I just couldn't allow UL to continue as they had been without any competition. I wouldn't accept that. UL probably figured that they had to finally allow me to gain recognition After going through so many obstacles and delays with government, if UL was actually responsible for all the delays, they had to feel that they accomplished their goals. Delaying a competitor from entering a closed market for over fifteen years would be a big accomplishment in anybody's book. But they knew that the real problem of MET entering this business was just starting. Many of the reasons for the delay were of my own making. I didn't aggressively pursue OSHA, I took too long to hire an experienced legal counsel, and I allowed inaction by the government to drag on for a year or more. But mostly, I didn't recognize or accept the fact that the task was too big for me to handle alone. I was so used to doing everything on my own. Why would this need to be different? So at the end of the day, I have to blame myself.

Everything we needed to accomplish to get customers for the product safety business was handed to UL many years ago. I didn't think we could run fast enough to catch up. All we could do was keep running and keep trying, but like a dog in a dog track, the rabbit was always a little ahead. I wondered if the dog ever figured that the rabbit couldn't be caught. Did I need to accept the fact that the rabbit couldn't be caught? At what point was I expected to decide that there were too many obstacles to overcome?

What I had to do was to look for new business in markets where UL was not or approval by the local jurisdictions was required. When I was at home Marcia would say "Why beat your head against a wall? You have a fairly good business. Do you need all this aggravation?"

The laboratory business we had was making money, and Marcia was right, but I couldn't just give up. That's not my way; I'm a fighter. To give up after all I had been through meant I was accepting defeat. If the fight hadn't been so long and had I not gone as far as I did, maybe I would have thrown in the towel, but I was in way too deep to give up. I was ready to see this thing through.

Every challenge I've overcome in my life, I always get through it. Becoming a design engineer, a pilot, a certified professional engineer—I accomplished it all with pure determination. As a child, I never played sports. Physically I had real limitations, and I knew it; it wasn't hard for me to accept. But I realized early on that I could use my brain to make major strides in life. They say knowledge is power, and I couldn't agree more. Even with my lack of formal education, if the knowledge I need is in a book or is available elsewhere and I can access it, I'll learn it, and I'll find a way to reach my goals. Don't tell me I'm not qualified or not acceptable; that will only make me want it more.

Now I was faced with the problem of contacting over ten thousand municipalities, and nothing from my past experience prepared me to handle it. It seemed impossible. Could this be the one that's out of my reach? For me, it wasn't a question of "How do I do this?" or "Can I do this?" It was a question of "Where do I start?" and "What do I do first?" And the answers weren't in any book I could reference or person I could call.

I would lie in bed and ask myself, *What am I going to do?* This was where I got my best ideas. More than once I went into the office in the morning, facing a big problem without a plan or idea; and I'd say to myself, *Just do something. Anything. Just do something!* More often than not, it helped or at least gave me a good start. I thought I would receive calls from companies ready to send us their business. I thought my next problem would be how to handle all the business we would be getting. But that didn't happen. That would have been too easy. So in order to have all the jurisdictions recognize us, we pursued another strategy: we took one state at time, jurisdiction by jurisdiction, and kept going, waiting for another miracle. It wasn't a very good business plan—a lot of prayer and waiting for a miracle—but I wasn't quitting.

CHAPTER TWENTY

Following the lawsuit, the law requiring an NRTL label was now the law of the land, all electrical products installed or used in the United States had to be tested and listed by a nationally recognized testing laboratory (NRTL), not just UL. All products that are installed in a workplace fall under the jurisdiction of OSHA. In contrast, products installed in a home fall under the jurisdiction of a designated, local electrical inspector. Therefore, a manufacturer of any electrical product needs approval of all jurisdictions because they may not know where they will ultimately be installed.

There are basically two classes of products that a manufacturer would want to submit to a lab for certification: a completed one-of-a-kind product or a sample of a product that is made in larger quantities for mass production.

A one-of-a-kind product would be something like an automatic car wash. It is made to particular specifications depending on the needs of the client. A product like this is tested to the same product standard as other machines, but that car wash will receive a unique and specific certification that applies only to that product. On this one product, the testing company or the manufacturer will contact the specific jurisdiction where the car wash is to be installed and receive permission to accept it there.

Other products that are manufactured for mass production are tested differently: example a home toaster oven In this case, one sample of the toaster is submitted to the lab and is tested in accordance with the standards. If the test is successful and the manufacturer signs a contract ensuring that each subsequent toaster will be manufactured exactly the same as the original, then the manufacturer is given permission to mass produce that toaster. The manufacturer must also agree to allow periodic unannounced inspections at his plant to ensure he is following the guidelines. No changes of any kind are allowed on the product without prior approval. He also must have in place a quality control system that helps ensure the continued compliance with the standard for the product. For products like this, the manufacturer needs to ensure that, wherever the product is sold in the United States, it also meets the requirements of the local jurisdiction.

MET had been working for over thirty years to test and approve the custom one-of-a-kind products that were not destined for mass distribution, such as the car wash These products only required approval from the local inspection jurisdiction, and that's when they would call us. At the time,

OSHA did not have regulations on these items. We had been very successful in this area and had established MET as a reputable and recognized field inspection organization in and around the Maryland area.

By the time I won the lawsuit, there were about one thousand jurisdictions that were familiar with our work and had experience with us; but in order to test products for mass distribution, I would need approval of all U.S. jurisdictions, which meant there were still about nine thousand more to go.

The strategy was to contact most of them, or at least the ones that mattered. With code authorities, there are certain inspectors who are active with the National Electrical Code and/or the International Electrical Inspectors Association (IAEI). These inspection groups have regular meetings throughout the United States to discuss national issues and provide training functions for inspectors on the National Electrical Code, knowing the code is a requirement for all inspectors since they are required to enforce it.

In every municipality, there's at least one inspector who is considered more involved with these groups. He or she attends meetings, is up-to-date on code and inspection issues, and is generally a focal point for other inspectors within the jurisdiction for code or application questions. While there were many inspectors who had never heard of the lawsuit and did not know how OSHA affected their operation, this chief inspector knew the issue very well because it was often a topic at meetings, and the inspector would disseminate the information to all the other inspectors who did not attend the meetings.

We thought the best way to obtain acceptance of MET in all jurisdictions was to concentrate our efforts on contacting all these key inspectors. We started in Oregon. At the time, we had MET-certified product that was being rejected by the inspection authority there, so we knew that opening up that market would be the most beneficial to us.

The chief electrical inspector in Oregon was very knowledgeable and up to date on issues. I contacted him and offered to fly him to Baltimore and show him around our laboratory. Turns out, an all-expense- paid trip is a hard offer to turn down. A week later, the inspector was standing in our lab, asking poignant questions about our standards, inspecting our equipment, and interviewing our engineers. His inspection was scrupulous, but in the end, he was impressed, and we passed easily. This was no small victory for us because it was our third state, following Maryland and Virginia, that was added to our list of state recognition. In states like Oregon, all jurisdictions trust the decisions of the chief inspector and rely on his or her opinion as to what should be acceptable in other jurisdictions within the state. So when we were approved by this inspector, we were also approved by all local jurisdictions within Oregon.

Although the ultimate decision lies with each local inspector, if there was an individual inspector in a state that had the ability to recommend approval or acceptance of certification from a lab, we attempted to obtain that inspector's approval, much like we did with Oregon. We furnished as much information as we could and anything else we could provide that might be needed by the state to accept our certification. If we needed to pay an individual to visit our lab and personally see our facility, we'd do it gladly. And we did many times. In addition to Oregon, we invited the chief inspectors from Washington State, North Carolina, and others.

In some jurisdictions, cities had requirements that we needed to deal with individually, which was more work that I had to take on, and I wasn't pleased to deal with individual cities; there were just too many of them, but we couldn't afford to be rejected anywhere. Not being recognized by even one small jurisdiction could prevent a manufacturer from using MET as it would disrupt their marketing and sales strategy. And I couldn't blame any manufacturer for choosing UL over MET when the selection was critical to them selling their products and ultimately their success.

If we failed to gain acceptance everywhere, UL would continue to maintain their dominance. At this time we were the only entity that could prevent UL's continued monopoly. If nothing else, that's what we are going to do.

CHAPTER TWENTY-ONE

Product testing requires performing a series of required tests in accordance with a standard or specification.

The extent of these standards is extraordinary. Imagine all the electrical products in your home: your hairdryer, your phone charger, your computer, lamps, plug-in kitchen devices. Within each product category, there are dozens, if not hundreds, of other products that compete with the one you own. For each of *those* products, there are standards that describe the tests that must be performed to ensure that product is safe for you and not only the ones in your home but medical devices, factory equipment, and office electronics. There are literally thousands of tests that a lab needs to be able to perform.

The standards are fairly easy to obtain; they are available from a variety of sources. The problem arises when acquiring the appropriate test equipment. Testing requires the use of specialized equipment that is specifically designed for laboratory use. Some of the test equipment was readily available from electronic manufactures, but it was very specialized to perform a specific test. The only people that would have a need for such equipment are the test labs or, in some instances, the manufacturer of the item. Since UL had been the only universally approved test lab for so long that they were essentially the only customer for a testing equipment manufacturer.

Prior to winning the lawsuit, no lab or company other than UL had ever needed to perform the tests described in a product standard. Although some manufacturers would perform a test on the product before they submitted the product to a lab, there was never much of a demand for this incredibly specific test equipment.

When I started out, I worked tirelessly in my home to build the equipment needed for testing. Night after night, while Marcia washed the dirtied dishes from supper, I would retire to my basement to construct elaborate pieces of test equipment. Not only was it cheaper, but many times it was the only way to acquire a necessary device.

Back then, UL was the only lab performing these tests, so they were the only lab that had the equipment. It wasn't until we entered this business that there was a need for someone other than UL to have the equipment. Now I needed it.

Fortunately this was not a problem for me. I had the ability and the experience of building test equipment for field testing. I now had to build equipment to test hundreds of products to meet hundreds of product safety standards. This was no small feat; most of the equipment was relatively large and heavy. Not as large as a 3000 pound load bank, luckily, but large enough that they had to be placed on wheels so they could be moved around the lab. Many pieces of testing equipment required that I have a shop and a machinist, two assets that turned out to be invaluable for the business. With the exception of some transformers and certain electronic circuits, I personally designed and engineered almost everything we had to build.

For smaller items, I returned to my trusted basement. It became customary for me to spend a few hours a night in my basement workshop, building the equipment I could easily transport to the lab. If a device was too large or heavy, I would work on the control portion at home, then take that part to the lab, and connect it to the heavy part.

The requirements for testing were endless. As we were getting recognized for more standards and approved to test a wider range of products, the requirements for testing equipment kept increasing. I spent more than half my time designing and building special testing equipment that couldn't be purchased anywhere in the world.

Every test that we needed to perform, UL had already done. I could no longer tell people that we had the ability to perform tests that no one else did, as had been the case when we were performing field tests. Moreover, when UL wrote a standard for a new test, the test usually involved an item of testing equipment they already owned; they didn't have to bother with obtaining new equipment.

We were always in catch-up mode, but we dealt with it. I always knew, without a doubt, that we could do any test UL could write a standard for, and we were tested on this many times. When UL wrote a standard for testing products used in an explosive atmosphere, we designed and built a chamber to perform this test in accordance with the standard. We filled the chamber with an explosive mixture of hydrogen and set off an explosion to test the device. I went to a scrap yard in Baltimore where I bought a hatch from a naval ship. I had our machinist weld it in to seal the chamber. A lot of effort, but it worked and we did the test to the standard. When the Mine Safety and Health Administration (MSHA) came to inspect our chamber, the inspector told me how impressed he was with it.

The market was opening up. Now, more laboratories were getting into the testing business, which meant more opportunities for a specialty manufacturer to start offering testing equipment like the kind I had been building for years. As in most free market societies, the market was stepping up to satisfy a need. Not only did my suit open the market for competition with test laboratories, it also created opportunities for manufacturers of testing equipment because it was no longer just UL doing the testing. Many labs didn't have the ability to build their own test equipment, so opening up this market was their ticket in the door.

Also, many NRTLs were testing products manufactured by American companies to be sold in Europe. These products needed to be tested to either European standards or international standards, which were slightly different from the U.S. standards. European connection plugs had different voltages than American ones. All this resulted in needing more testing equipment to accommodate the foreign standards. Many of the items we found were easier to build ourselves, but often we did buy from a few of the new manufacturers that were emerging in this market.

There was no doubt that the emergence of this market was necessary to the evolution of the testing field. With more players in the game, there was more opportunity for competition, which is a cornerstone of the free market. But I truly loved building my own equipment. In later years, when there were no more fights for recognition, I retired to my basement shop at home where I would resort to doing what I really enjoyed: designing and building special testing equipment.

CHAPTER TWENTY-TWO

Pursuing state jurisdiction approval one at a time made a lot of sense, but that alone wouldn't work. There are many cities and other smaller jurisdictions that are not required to accept the decision of their state chief inspector. Los Angeles was one of those jurisdictions. We learned that Los Angeles had a requirement to approve labs, and we weren't on their approval list. I really didn't want to start dealing with individual cities, especially ones on the other side of the country; but we were in no position to allow MET to slip through the cracks, even in one municipality. The state of California didn't have a central approval body, so we were forced to deal with the city of Los Angles itself.

I contacted the city to get a copy of their requirements, probably the only request of this kind they had ever received (I assume they developed the requirements just for us because of this). One of these requirements was a personal visit by their inspection authority, all expenses paid. Again, we had to agree to this, but I couldn't afford to keep this up for every jurisdiction. There are just too many of them.

I called the chief electrical inspector of Los Angeles, Bob Bassman.

"We need your approval to be recognized in Los Angeles."

"In order for that to happen, it is mandatory that I personally inspect your laboratory."

"Yes, I read the requirements, and I will gladly pay your expenses to come out here and visit us at MET."

We agreed to a date, and he flew out a week later to inspect our facilities. I was sure we were going to pass his inspection. He immediately started by telling me, "Don't tell me anything about NRTLs. I'm not interested in that," he insisted shortly upon his arrival to the MET lab. "We will do our own inspection with our requirements and make our own decisions."

This initial attitude really worried me. Is he mad because I didn't pick him up at the airport? Or because I didn't make the right hotel reservations?

Turns out, that was just the way he made his first impression. He went through our lab for two days, tying our engineers up with loads of questions the entire time. Naturally, he repeated much of what had already been done previously by other experts, but he needed to do it all over again for himself on behalf of Los Angeles.

"Well, everything's acceptable here. You'll be receiving an official letter shortly," he declared on the final day of his visit. It was as I had expected. I didn't mind the inspection and the time involved, but if we had to go through this for many more of the jurisdictions, we wouldn't get any work done and would have to shut down.

Most of the cities we contacted treated us with respect; our phone calls or letters were always answered promptly. We have to credit this to our relationship with the local electrical inspectors and our activity with the International Association of Electrical Inspectors (IAEI). The publicity we received from our OSHA accreditation surely helped. We attended all the electrical inspector meetings and set up a booth at these meetings where we handed out literature on MET and spoke one-on-one with as many inspectors as we could. We called or visited many cities and were received very professionally.

The city of Chicago, though, was a different story. They didn't return phone calls or letters requesting an appointment. When I called and spoke with a secretary, she usually said, "I'll forward the message to the chief inspector and he will call you back." He never did. I couldn't allow a big city like Chicago to refuse to accept MET.

I discussed this problem with Melvin who gave me his favorite answer, "If all else fails, sue." I dreaded another court fight. Luckily I wasn't the only lab Chicago was treating this way. Dash, Straus & Goodhue was a lab led by a good friend of mine Glen Dash, a partner in the lab and a great attorney. He saw the need and was willing to take on the fight.

In early 1990, after officially being denied recognition by the city, Glen Dash filed a lawsuit in the United States district court in Northern District, Illinois, against the city of Chicago. The city felt it had reasonable grounds to deny Dash recognition. Chicago, as well as OSHA, has a requirement that in order for the laboratory to be independent it must engage in "no other business" besides testing.

Dash publishes a magazine used by the industry called *Compliance Engineering*, which accepts advertisements from manufacturers and other companies in the industry. The magazine is devoted to safety standards and related technical matters. The city of Chicago determined that Dash's publication of the magazine violated the code's requirement that a lab not be in any other business besides testing. Dash challenged the city of Chicago's refusal to approve it as an electrical testing laboratory on four grounds:

Dash alleged that the OSHA Act preempts the code pursuant to the supremacy clause of article 6 of the Federal Constitution.

Dash alleged that the city's refusal to approve it as a testing laboratory violates its rights under the equal protection clause of the fourteenth amendment of the Federal Constitution.

Dash contended that the city's delegation of absolute accreditation authority to an administrative agency without clear standards to govern its accreditation authority violated the due process clause of the fourteenth amendment of the Federal Constitution.

Dash asserted that, assuming arguendo the testing laboratory provisions are constitutional, it meets the requirements for accreditation set forth in these provisions and seeks a mandatory injunction and/or a writ of mandamus ordering the city to approve it as an electrical testing laboratory.

Through lengthy court challenges and arguments detailing Dash's and the city of Chicago's position, Dash won, and the city of Chicago was enjoined from regulating the Dash-approved electrical products in OSHA-regulated workplaces. Of course, Glen Dash's win was also a win for us, and we proceeded to hear less about the rejection of MET Laboratories.

Chicago was a big step toward obtaining approvals from municipalities. Any city that still had illusions about blocking MET without a substantial reason had to think twice. Dash's win must have convinced cities not to try. If Dash had lost the suit, UL would have tried to influence as many jurisdictions as they could to reject Dash and then MET.

We felt we could now confidently claim complete acceptance of our laboratory and our certification mark everywhere in the United States. It was a major accomplishment by any standards, going from one thousand jurisdictions' acceptance to all ten thousand. But I knew that we weren't finished climbing. There was still one more wall to climb, and this next one was big. We didn't know exactly where to start and how to be convincing enough to cause our new clients to change what they have been comfortable with for many years. There would be no one to sue or challenge to overcome this obstacle: I now needed to convince the large retailers like Home Depot and Lowe's to accept electrical products with the MET certification. These companies have the freedom to buy what they want, and they could not to be coerced to buy anything they felt would not accelerate their business.

I dreaded the problem of needing to convince a retailer to accept a product if they didn't want to, just because it had a MET certification mark. On this issue I couldn't contemplate a solution. Back to not knowing what I could do, but keep moving forward.

CHAPTER TWENTY-THREE

After clearing all the hurdles we had encountered over the past twenty years or so, I wondered, "How could there still be more? When is this going to end?"

There wasn't a problem obtaining manufacturing customers. We offered great advantages over UL to manufacturers. What we needed was to have the products we certified accepted and purchased by retailers. Large retailers didn't have an issue with MET performing the certification. Their concern was only whether it would affect their sales. We managed to draw in many new manufacturers, both large and small, who were ready to go with us. But the problem was that these manufacturers needed to be able to sell their products to retailers.

Going from one major undertaking to another was starting to take a toll on me. I was losing my "I can do anything" attitude, and my confidence was suffering. Whenever I was having a tough time or doubting myself, I knew I could turn to John Stevens. He understood the situation and was always willing to listen and shell out sound advice. "Let's sit and plan out how you have to tackle this new problem," he said. "Don't just respond. Let's have a plan! Have you ever heard of any business that took over twenty years to be accepted? Not just to get established but allowed to simply operate?"

"Had I thought of what it would take, I don't think I would have done it," I replied. "I know my family suffered for all the time I devoted to this business. Even on family vacations, my time wasn't entirely devoted to the vacation. I would leave everyone to work on a job or find a phone where I could slip away and call in."

I was now at a point where all the suffering they endured could be repaid to them from my success. By now, my children were grown and had families of their own. I wanted to schedule my time better to be home with Marcia and see my children and grandchildren.

But convincing retailers to sell MET products was my last hurdle—I was sure of it—and I needed to clear this obstacle before I could consider myself victorious. This kind of effort, I convinced myself, wouldn't be as demanding on my time as getting MET established, although I still had priorities at the lab, designing and building test equipment for ourselves.

I aimed high when contacting retailers. We didn't need every retailer to accept us—just a few—then it would snowball into acceptance from other retailers. I hoped! So I started with the leaders in the industry and my ideal retailers: Home Depot and Lowe's.

The major issue these companies expressed was that they didn't want customers asking "Who is MET?" when buying a product or to feel that a product without a UL mark was in some way inferior. I had to keep pushing wherever an opportunity existed to get the MET mark on products. I created a set of talking points to convince the large retailers that if a MET-certified product arrived in their store it would sell, and the certification would have little or no effect. If the product met the approval of the customer, it would sell without question, and my goal was to convince these large retailers that the customer would approve.

It's difficult to find the right person in a large corporation, especially since I didn't know what department to start with. When I called Home Depot, the telephone operators were very helpful and politely passed me from one person to another until I reached Steve Howard in product quality assurance. I quickly learned that the right department in these types of stores was the quality assurance department.

"Hi, My name is Len Frier with an independent testing company called MET," I introduced myself.
"Hello, Mr. Frier. How can I be of service to you?"
"Well, I'd like to schedule an appointment with you to discuss

the possibility of Home Depot selling electrical products with a certification mark that is an alternative to UL."

"An alternative?" he inquired.

"Yes, we have recently been accredited to test and certify products to all national standards and local codes and provides our own certification for those products. The certification mark we provide is acceptable throughout the United States. I would like to meet with you and explain the benefits of allowing MET-certified products in your stores."

He listened to my sales pitch very politely, and we set up a meeting for the following week.

"This is so much easier than just finding the right person to talk to in a government agency," I thought. Almost immediately after hanging up the phone with Home Depot, I gave a ring to the quality assurance department at Lowe's Home Improvement Warehouse. I spoke with Mr. John Istwan, the director of quality assurance for Lowe's. Again, I introduced myself and gave the spiel.

And after listening to me for a few minutes, he responded, "I respect what you're doing, Mr. Frier, but unfortunately at this time, we exclusively require UL certification."

"I understand that, but if you just give me a couple of minutes of your time to meet with you, I know I can show you that there are manufacturers that are having trouble using UL, and they really have good products." I couldn't afford to take no for an answer. I stood firm and surprised myself with how confident I sounded.

"Ok, I like where you're coming from, so how about we set up a meeting for next week? I can't make any promises, though."

Ecstatic and jittery, I thanked him, hung up the phone, and started preparations for two of the biggest meetings of my career, the culmination of my efforts for the past twenty years, I thought. If these companies wouldn't accept MET, we were dead. There was no one to argue with, no one to sue if they said no. My fate was in the hands of a few individuals at these stores. The more I realized how important this presentation was, the more I worried.

The headquarters for both companies are located a short flight apart, so I decided to tackle both meetings in one trip. This is where owning a plane was a real asset.

The day of my Home Depot meeting, I flew myself down to a private airport on the west side of Atlanta. I rented a car and made it to their offices about a half hour before my appointment time. The waiting area was full of suppliers waiting to talk to buyers, everyone hopeful that their product would land on the shelves of this massive retailer.

I nervously approached the receptionist. "I'm here to meet with Mr. Howard," I said.

She looked at the appointment schedule, and without looking up, she asked, "Len Frier?"

"Yes."

She made a check mark next to my name in bold black ink.

"I'll get Mr. Howard for you," she said politely. "Just have a seat."

In no more than five minutes, Mr. Howard came out and introduced himself, and we made our way to the conference room.

Four gentlemen, not much older than me, all sat around a large glass top conference table, anxiously awaiting my presentation.

I was hoping I would be the one in the driver's seat, but before I could say a word, they started asking me about the lawsuit and MET's journey to get recognized.

"We have been keeping a close watch on what is happening around the country with regard to approval of electrical products," said Mr. Howard, "so we're very glad you paid us a visit."

I graciously responded to all their questions until they had nothing else to ask. Then one gray-haired gentleman said, "You can go ahead and begin your presentation, Len."

I had a PowerPoint presentation prepared for them. It had taken me all week to perfect, up until the night before when I stayed up putting the final touches on it. So when it came time to present, of course, the computer wasn't cooperating. I fiddled with it for about two minutes, wanting nothing more than to jump out the nearest window.

"I'm so sorry, but something seems to be malfunctioning." I explained, humiliated.

"Don't worry, we can make copies," Mr. Howard responded. "Technology is not always the most reliable."

He called in his assistant who promptly made five copies of my presentation, and I worked from that. Aside from the technical difficulties, the presentation went very well.

As Mr. Howard walked me to the elevators, he said, "Unless there are any issues with our attorneys, I could see no reason why Home Depot wouldn't accept products with the MET mark."

With a great feeling about Home Depot's acceptance and a boost of confidence, I flew that afternoon direct to Wilkesboro, North Carolina, so I would be fresh the next morning to meet with Lowe's. That night, alone in my hotel room, I wondered if I would receive the same reception as Home Depot. I drifted off to sleep, knowing this long journey was soon coming to an end, and I was excited for everything that lay ahead.

The next morning, I visited the Lowe's headquarters where I only met with John Istwan, my contact in the quality assurance department. It became clear that these retailers had a different attitude toward vendors than the government agencies I had visited. It appeared that these folks really were interested in what I had to offer, whereas the government had felt we were creating additional work for them.

This time the computer worked perfectly as I delivered the same presentation I had at Home Depot.

"Many jurisdictions have consumer protection laws that require products to be listed, and nearly all jurisdictions accept a MET certification," I explained.

"Is there a way I can see a copy of these laws?" he asked.

"Sure, I'll make a package of those and send them to you when I return to Baltimore."

"Could you also send me details on the specific jurisdictions where MET is recognized?"

"Absolutely," I said.

John listened intently showed a sincere interest in the new NRTL mark, which was something I never received from the government.

I left the Lowe's meeting and flew home that evening. Back in Baltimore, I packaged up some of these laws and a copy of the OSHA NRTL requirements to send to him. I also told him that North Carolina was one of those states with consumer protection laws and gave him the name of the right contact and the phone number for their offices in Raleigh. He told me he would be meeting with his attorneys in late December and should have an answer shortly after that.

In December, he contacted me again, this time with a letter stating that Lowe's was revising their policy to allow accredited laboratories other than UL to certify products sold in their stores. That was my victory stamp. MET was approved by the biggest name retailers, and I couldn't have been happier.

My next major target was Sears Roebuck in Chicago. Maybe I was naive in thinking that all these meetings would go as smoothly as the first two. But I still had some obstacles in store for me. I found the name of the contact person relatively fast: Mr. George Zelazny, the manager of product safety. I called him several times and left messages with his secretary, but he never returned my calls. What I failed to realize at the time was that I was in Chicago, a nearby neighbor of the UL headquarters in Northbrook, Illinois. In Chicago it was much easier for UL to exert their influence on a major company in their own backyard, just neighbors helping neighbors. My dealings in Chicago were completely different from what I experienced everywhere else. No matter what I did, I got nowhere. Could it be the UL connection? I wondered.

I finally wrote to Alan Lacy, chairman and president of Sears. After a few weeks, I received an e-mail from Gene Ostap in the product quality assurance department. His response was that Sears would only accept UL and wasn't going to change. He was unyielding, and there wasn't much else I could do. I just had to hope that a manufacturer with a MET-certified product would approach Sears and Sears would want to sell that product. Several years later, I was browsing the shelves at Sears when I came across a few products with a MET label. I was pleased to find that Sears had changed its policy and allowed other products into their stores. At that moment, I knew I had cleared that final hurdle, conquered the last wall, built and sustained a booming company amid extreme opposition. And it felt great.

As time passed, my son Robert became more active in MET and eventually assumed the role of president. He then took on the responsibility of acquiring major retailers to sell MET products, following up with Home Depot and eventually securing Best Buy and Walmart. He expanded MET's international influence as well, opening laboratories in China and Korea where many manufacturers are based. Being close to the manufacturer is essential in getting their business. He is a hard worker, loyal and dedicated, and I can't think of a better man than Robert to continue where I left off and lead MET into the future.

When I look back at all my efforts, failures, and successes, I see there was much of each. My successes opened a large market for hundreds of people in a profitable and rewarding field, providing competition in an ever-expanding world. The secret, I found, is to have more successes than failures. But in any stage in life, it's hard to know where our efforts are leading. I don't think we can see clearly which effort will be a success and which will be a failure. I never look and any issue negatively and always tried to move in a positive direction. I dedicated myself to my goal, and that is how, I assume, I did succeed. When there is integrity in your work, you never have to look back at something you've done and worry. You move forward with peace of mind. Devotion, hard work, and honesty are the elements of success—at least the elements of my success. I never looked at any of these walls as too much for me conquer. I just went forward with hope, one small step, at a time and eventually reached my goal. And it was all worth it.

CPSIA information can be obtained at www.ICGtesting.com
Printed in the USA
BVOW08*1017220415

397262BV00011B/115/P